5
NIGHTS A
WEEK

BY VALLI LITTLE

delicious.

Every recipe you'll ever need for midweek cooking

contents

With the busy lives we lead, there's less and less time for planning, shopping and preparing weeknight meals. Not to mention the fact that it can be hard to come up with new and exciting ideas for dinner which won't take hours in the kitchen.

So it's not hard to understand why many **delicious.** readers tell us that they love the fact that so many of our pages are filled with fun fuss-free dishes that are perfect for midweek cooking. In **5 Nights a Week** we have brought together flavours from around the world and translated them into creative family meals, including easy pastas, speedy curries and satisfying salads. Plus, vegetarian dishes and low-fat options that are great for the family but are also impressive enough for when you have friends over for midweek dinners.

5 Nights a Week, our latest cookbook, has been designed to help you to balance your busy schedule with your love of good food. And because they are **delicious.** recipes, you can be confident that they have been rigorously tested, are easy to follow and use readily available ingredients.

There are no elaborate techniques or esoteric ingredients, just **good home cooking** that **everyone will love.**

It has been great fun putting this collection together – I've even rediscovered some old favourites to cook for my own family in the process. I hope it will inspire you, too, so that dinner becomes something you really look forward to preparing, cooking and eating every night of the week.

Happy cooking,

Valli

delicious. essentials

cooking the delicious. way

To help you get the best results from these recipes, here are some useful tips:

Before you start cooking, read the complete recipe, gather the ingredients and prepare them as stated in the recipe list (such as peeling, chopping, etc.).

Unless stated otherwise, butter is unsalted; eggs are 60g; sugar is caster; garlic, onions and ginger are peeled; and fresh herbs and salad greens are washed and dried.

top gear

By this, I mean make sure you have essential cooking equipment, including:

• A large, heavy-based frying pan or casserole (one that can go into the oven, too, will be a great asset).

• A set of good-quality saucepans and a griddle pan.

• A good set of electric scales and a set of measuring cups and spoons.

• At least two good knives (and sharpen them frequently).

• A good pepper mill – freshly ground black pepper is always the best.

• Good-quality baking trays. By that I mean ones that don't buckle when you put them in a hot oven (although I do sometimes use disposable foil trays when making lasagnes and pasta bakes).

• Finally, a food processor and KitchenAid mixer – for me, they are a cook's best friends!

shopping

Make a list! There is nothing worse than getting home only to discover that you have forgotten that all-too-vital ingredient. Separate the items into categories i.e. meat, dairy, fruit and vegetables, etc. It makes it so much easier when you are whizzing around the supermarket.

Or shop online. It is so easy to order online these days and get your groceries delivered, leaving small items to be picked up locally.

my store cupboard

Keep a well-stocked store cupboard. Keep a list posted on the door indicating when things are running low so you can add them to your next shopping list. I have listed opposite my store cupboard staples, but feel free to add your own personal favourites. Don't forget to include condiments such as onion marmalade, tapenade, quince paste and aïoli, which are all readily available these days and can turn a simple meal into something quite special. Check your cupboards regularly and throw out any out-of-date items. Adopt a use-it-or-lose-it policy.

here are the staples I always have on hand:

in the cupboard
Asian noodles
Asian sauces
  hoisin sauce
  kecap manis (Indonesian sweet soy)
  oyster sauce
  light and dark soy sauce
  Thai fish sauce
Canned coconut milk
Canned pulses
  borlotti beans
  cannellini beans
  chickpeas
  lentils
Canned tomatoes
Canned tuna – good-quality, in oil
Chinese rice wine (shaohsing)
Couscous
Curry pastes and powder
Dijon mustard
Dried herbs and spices
Dried pasta – all shapes and sizes
Dried shiitake and porcini mushrooms
Mango chutney
Mirin (Japanese cooking wine)
Oil
  olive (regular for cooking and
    extra virgin for drizzling over
    salads and vegetables)
  peanut (for stir-fries)
  sesame (for flavouring Asian dishes)
Pesto – red and green
Preserved lemons
Rice
  arborio
  basmati
  brown
  jasmine
Sea salt

Stock
  beef
  chicken
  fish
  vegetable
Sweet chilli sauce
Tomato sauce (ketchup)
Tomato passata (sugo)
Vinegar
  balsamic
  red wine
  sherry
  white wine

in the fridge/freezer
Butter (French, when I can afford it)
Eggs – free-range
Fresh herbs – even if they are in a
  small pot on the windowsill
Frozen peas
Natural yoghurt
Olives
Parmesan
Pastry
  puff pastry sheets
  ready-rolled shortcrust
Ricotta cheese
Vanilla ice cream – the best you
  can afford

and finally, the essentials
Freshly ground coffee
Red and white wine (some for the
  pot and some for me)
Tea (leaves, not bags)

5 nights a week
soups

macadamia nut soup

450g unsalted macadamia nuts,
    roughly chopped
3 potatoes, peeled and chopped
1 large leek, white part only,
    washed, sliced
1 onion, peeled, chopped
1 litre chicken stock
300ml thick cream
toasted baguette slices, to serve

Preheat the oven to 180°C/350°F/gas mark 4.

Place 2 heaped tablespoons of the nuts on a tray and roast until golden. Set aside. Place the potato, leek, onion and stock in a large saucepan and bring to the boil. Reduce heat to low and simmer for 20 minutes, or until the potato is soft. Set aside to cool slightly.

Add the remaining macadamia nuts and blend in batches until smooth. Stir in the cream and season with salt and pepper. Serve chilled or hot, garnished with the roasted nuts and slices of toasted baguette.

Serves 6

pistou soup

40ml olive oil
1 leek (white part only), finely chopped
1 carrot, cut into 1cm cubes
1 large potato, peeled, cut into
    1cm cubes
500ml chicken or vegetable stock
1 tomato, peeled, seeds removed,
    cut into 1cm cubes
420g can four-bean mix,
    drained, rinsed
50g thin French or thin green beans,
    ends trimmed, cut into 2cm lengths
1 large courgette, chopped
5 tbsp good-quality basil pesto
slices of chargrilled bread or baguette,
    to serve

Heat the oil in a large saucepan, add the leek and sweat over a low heat for 1–2 minutes. Add the carrot and potato and cook, stirring, for a further minute. Add the stock and 250ml water and bring to the boil. Reduce heat, simmer for 5 minutes, then add the tomato, four-bean mix, French or green beans and courgette. Season with salt and pepper. Cook for a further 2 minutes, stir in half the pesto, then ladle into serving bowls. Add a dollop of the remaining pesto and serve with slices of chargrilled bread.

Serves 4

spiced **carrot** soup with **coconut cream**

20ml light olive oil
1 onion, finely chopped
2 garlic cloves, crushed
1 small red chilli, seeds
    removed, chopped
1 tsp grated fresh ginger
500g carrots, chopped
1 sweet potato (kumara),
    peeled, chopped
2 kaffir lime leaves*
1 litre chicken stock
juice of ½ lime
2 heaped tbsp palm sugar*
40ml Thai fish sauce
200ml coconut cream
150ml thick cream
grated nutmeg (optional), to serve

Heat the oil in a saucepan over medium heat, add the onion and cook for 2–3 minutes, or until softened. Add the garlic, chilli, ginger, carrot, sweet potato, lime leaves and stock. Bring to the boil, then reduce heat to low and simmer for 20 minutes.

Allow to cool slightly, then purée in a blender. Pass the purée through a sieve, then season. Return to the pan with the lime juice, sugar and fish sauce and gently reheat. Whip the creams until thick. Pour the soup into glasses and top with the coconut cream and a sprinkle of nutmeg, if desired.

* Kaffir lime leaves are available from selected greengrocers and Asian food shops. Palm sugar is available from Asian food shops.

Serves 6–8

minted **pea soup** with **smoked salmon** & **cream cheese** toasts

20g unsalted butter
1 tsp olive oil
1 small white onion, chopped
1kg frozen peas
500ml chicken stock
60g mint leaves
4 thick slices rustic bread,
   toasted
cream cheese, to spread
8 slices smoked salmon
4 tbsp natural yoghurt, to serve

Heat the butter and olive oil in a large, deep saucepan over a low heat. Add the chopped onion and cook, stirring, for about 5 minutes, until softened. Add the peas and stir gently to coat. Add the chicken stock and 500ml water. Increase the heat to high and bring to the boil, then add three-quarters of the mint leaves. In two batches, place the soup in a blender and blend to a thick purée. If necessary, return the soup to the cleaned saucepan and return to a medium heat until warmed through. Season generously.

Spread the toast with cream cheese and top with slices of smoked salmon.

Divide the soup among serving bowls, swirl a tablespoon of natural yoghurt through each, then sprinkle with freshly ground black pepper and the remaining mint leaves. Serve the soup with the smoked salmon toasts.

Serves 4

bean & tomato soup

20ml extra virgin olive oil
4 slices pancetta, chopped
1 leek (white part only), rinsed,
  finely chopped
1 carrot, finely chopped
1 heaped tbsp finely chopped fresh
  rosemary leaves
1 tsp tomato paste
410g canned crushed tomatoes
1¼ litres chicken stock
800g canned borlotti beans,
  drained, rinsed
16 cherry tomatoes on the vine, roasted
cheese sticks or grissini, to serve

Heat the oil in a large saucepan, then add the pancetta, leek, carrot and rosemary. Cook over low heat, stirring occasionally, for 5 minutes, until the vegetables soften. Add the tomato paste and cook for a further minute, then stir in the crushed tomatoes and stock. Bring to the boil and simmer for 10 minutes.

Add the borlotti beans and cook for a further 5 minutes. Cool slightly, remove 500ml of the soup and purée in a blender. Return to pan and stir with remaining soup.

Ladle into serving bowls and sit 4 roasted tomatoes in each. Serve with cheese sticks or grissini.

Serves 4

5 nights a week
salads

lamb & **mint** salad with potato croûtons

12 potatoes, boiled until
  just cooked, cooled
125ml olive oil
12 vine-ripened cherry tomatoes
20g mint leaves
50ml red wine vinegar
2 x 225g lamb loins
200g thin green beans, blanched
125g baby rocket leaves

Preheat the oven to 200°C/400°F/gas mark 6.

Using your hands, roughly break the potatoes into bite-sized pieces. Toss with a tablespoon of the olive oil, place on a baking tray and roast for 10 minutes, or until golden. Add the cherry tomatoes to the tray for the last 5 minutes of cooking. Remove from the oven and set aside.

Finely chop half the mint. Whisk together 80ml olive oil with the red wine vinegar, season with salt and pepper and stir in the chopped mint.

Heat the remaining oil in a non-stick frying pan over a high heat. Season the lamb with salt and pepper and seal on all sides in the pan. Reduce the heat to medium and cook for a further 2–3 minutes. The lamb should be just cooked but still rare inside. Set aside to rest.

Thinly slice the lamb when cool. In a large bowl, toss the lamb with the green beans, potato, tomatoes, rocket and remaining mint. Divide among serving plates and drizzle with dressing.

Serves 4

chicken & wild rice salad

300g jasmine and wild rice blend*
80ml mirin*
40ml rice vinegar
20ml tamari* or soy sauce
¼ tsp sesame oil
20ml lime juice
1 small red chilli, seeds removed,
  finely chopped
1 cucumber, halved, sliced on the diagonal
2 (380g total) cooked chicken breast fillets,
  finely shredded
3 tbsp chopped mint, plus extra leaves
  to garnish
3 tbsp chopped coriander, plus extra
  leaves to garnish
1 small red onion, very thinly sliced
75g chopped roasted peanuts
sweet chilli sauce and mixed salad
  leaves (optional), to serve

Cook the rice according to packet instructions. Drain, rinse in cold water, then drain again.

Place the mirin, vinegar, tamari, oil, juice and chilli in a large bowl. Add the cucumber, chicken, herbs, onion, peanuts and rice and toss to combine. Serve with extra herbs, sweet chilli sauce and lettuce leaves to wrap if desired.

* Available from selected supermarkets and Asian food shops.

Serves 6

taco salad with **sour cream** dressing

150ml sour cream
juice of ½ lemon
1 garlic clove, crushed
1 red onion, thinly sliced
1 cucumber, peeled,
  roughly chopped
500g cherry tomatoes, quartered
kernels from 4 cooked corn cobs
100g baby rocket leaves
230g plain corn chips

Whisk the sour cream, lemon juice and garlic with enough warm water (about 50ml) to form a smooth, loose dressing. Season and set aside.

Toss the remaining ingredients, except the chips, in a serving bowl. When ready to serve, toss through chips and dressing.

Serves 10

prawn caesar salad

2 baby cos lettuces, outer leaves discarded, roughly torn
500g cooked prawns, peeled, deveined, tails intact
4 rashers rindless bacon, cooked, chopped
200g toasted croûtons
20g grated Parmesan, plus extra to serve
125ml good-quality seafood cocktail sauce
40ml lemon juice
60ml crème fraîche
2 hard-boiled eggs, peeled, coarsely grated

Place the lettuce in a bowl with the prawns, bacon, croûtons and Parmesan. Mix the seafood sauce with the lemon juice, crème fraîche and 40ml of warm water, then season with salt and pepper. Add half the dressing to the salad and toss to combine. Pile the salad into serving bowls, drizzle with the remaining dressing and garnish with the grated egg and extra Parmesan.

Serves 4

warm squash & **goat's cheese** salad

½ small butterball squash or pumpkin
    (skin on), cut into thin wedges
100ml olive oil
20g thyme leaves
150g firm goat's cheese, cut into rounds
70g panko breadcrumbs*
2 tbsp balsamic vinegar
1 tsp Dijon mustard
250g mixed salad leaves

Preheat the oven to 200°C/400°F/gas mark 6.

Toss the squash with 40ml of the oil and the thyme.
Season with salt and freshly ground black pepper.
Place on a baking tray and roast for 30 minutes, turning
once, until cooked and lightly caramelised. Set aside to
cool slightly.

Meanwhile, brush the cheese rounds with 20ml of the
remaining olive oil and coat in the breadcrumbs. Place
on a separate greased baking tray and chill until just
before you're ready to serve the salad.

Whisk together the vinegar, mustard and remaining oil.
Season with salt and pepper.

Place the goat's cheese in the oven for 5–6 minutes,
until the crumbs are golden.

Toss the salad leaves and squash in half the vinaigrette
and pile onto plates. Add the warmed goat's cheese and
drizzle with the remaining vinaigrette.

* Available from Asian food shops. Substitute dry breadcrumbs.

Serves 4

5 nights a week
no-cook

lentil & brown rice salad

40ml red wine vinegar
80ml olive oil
1 tbsp Dijon mustard
400g can brown lentils, drained, rinsed
400g can borlotti beans, drained, rinsed
400g leftover cooked brown rice
1 small red onion, finely diced
2 Treviso radicchio (or regular
   radicchio), heart only
2 tomatoes, finely chopped
3 heaped tbsp chopped fresh tarragon
2 heaped tbsp chopped flat-leaf parsley

Whisk together the vinegar, oil and mustard in a small bowl, and season with salt and pepper.

Place the lentils, beans and rice in a large bowl with the onion. Finely shred one Treviso and add to the rice with the tomatoes, tarragon and parsley. Toss through the dressing and place on plates with remaining Treviso leaves.

Serves 4–6

christmas ploughman's

200g shredded cold cooked
   chicken or turkey
180g chopped ham
125g cream cheese
1 heaped tbsp chopped chives
275ml chicken consommé*
2 gelatine leaves*
8 pink peppercorns*
wedge of Cheddar, good-quality
   chutney, watercress leaves
   and crusty bread, to serve

Place the chicken or turkey, ham, cream cheese, chives and 100ml chicken consommé in a food processor, and process until smooth. Spoon into small serving dishes or one larger dish and smooth the top. Cover with plastic wrap and chill.

Place the remaining 175ml consommé in a saucepan over a medium heat until just below simmering point. Meanwhile, soak the gelatine leaves in cold water for 5 minutes to soften, then squeeze out excess water. Remove the consommé pan from the heat, add the gelatine and stir to dissolve. Allow to cool slightly.

Uncover the pâté and press the peppercorns onto the surface, then cover with a thin layer of the consommé mixture. Cover again and chill for 1 hour, or until jelly is firm.

Serve the pâté (it will keep in the fridge for 2–3 days) as part of a ploughman's lunch with Cheddar, chutney, watercress and crusty bread.

* Tetra packs of chicken consommé are available from selected supermarkets. Gelatine leaves are available from gourmet food shops. Always check the packet for setting instructions. Pink peppercorns in brine are available from gourmet food and spice shops; substitute dried black peppercorns.

Serves 4–6

mediterranean chicken & couscous salad

400g couscous
1 tsp chicken stock powder
40ml olive oil
100g good-quality whole
  egg mayonnaise
1 tsp smoked paprika (pimentón)*
2–3 (500g total) cooked chicken
  breasts, shredded
80g sliced marinated
  artichoke hearts
80g sliced roasted red pepper*
50g sliced semi-dried tomatoes
2 heaped tbsp chopped basil leaves,
  plus whole leaves to garnish
large lettuce leaves and lemon
  wedges (optional), to serve

Stir the couscous, stock powder and oil together in a large bowl, pour over 500ml boiling water, then cover with a tea towel and set aside for 10 minutes.

Meanwhile, combine the mayonnaise with the paprika in a large bowl. Add 40ml warm water to loosen, then toss with the chicken, artichoke, roasted pepper and tomatoes. Season to taste.

Fluff the couscous with a fork, season, then stir in the chopped basil. Pile the couscous and chicken into the lettuce leaves and scatter with basil leaves. Serve with lemon wedges, if desired.

*Smoked paprika is available from gourmet food shops and delis. Roasted pepper is available from delis and selected supermarkets.

Serves 4

deli plate

4–6 semi-dried tomatoes,
   or 3–4 vine-ripened cherry
   tomatoes
extra virgin olive oil, to drizzle
4 baby (cherry) bocconcini
¼ tsp dried red chilli flakes
¼ tsp dried basil
½ sliced roasted pepper*
1–2 thin prosciutto slices
2 marinated artichoke
   hearts, halved
about 8 black olives
grissini (such as rosemary), to serve

If using cherry tomatoes, preheat the oven to 180°C/350°F/gas mark 4.

Place the tomatoes on a baking tray, drizzle with oil and season with salt and pepper. Bake for 5 minutes, until the tomatoes just begin to soften. Remove and leave to cool.

Lightly roll two bocconcini in chilli and two in basil. Arrange all the ingredients on a plate, drizzle with extra virgin olive oil and season to taste.

* Roasted pepper is available from delis and selected supermarkets.

Serves 1

greek antipasto

200g tub taramasalata
80g marinated chilli peppers*
80g marinated kalamata olives
12 dolmades*
grilled lavash or pitta bread and lemon
   wedges, to serve

feta, tomato & cucumber salad
120g fresh oregano leaves
1 garlic clove, crushed
50ml olive oil
20ml lemon juice
250g Greek feta, sliced
125g cherry tomatoes, halved
1 cucumber, cut into chunks

Choose your own mix of marinated ingredients and fresh vegetables

For the salad, place the oregano, garlic, oil, lemon juice and 50ml warm water in a blender and process until smooth. Season with salt and pepper.

Place the feta, tomato and cucumber in a bowl and drizzle with the dressing, then serve, arranged on a platter, with the remaining ingredients.

* Marinated chillies are available from delis and Middle Eastern shops. Dolmades are tiny parcels of long-grain rice, toasted pine nuts, fresh herbs and seasoning, wrapped in vine leaves. They are available from delis and supermarkets.

Serves 4

5 nights a week
something on toast

blue cheese, prosciutto & rocket bruschetta

4 thick slices rustic bread
80ml extra virgin olive oil
1 garlic clove, halved
50ml balsamic vinegar
½ tsp brown sugar
80g wild rocket leaves
4 slices prosciutto
120g blue cheese, crumbled
10 walnuts, lightly toasted

Brush the bread with 20ml olive oil, and chargrill on a griddle, or grill for 1 minute, until golden. Turn over and cook for another minute, then rub one side with garlic.

Place the remaining oil, vinegar and sugar in a small bowl, season and whisk to combine. Toss the rocket with half the dressing. Top each slice of bread with a slice of prosciutto and rocket. Sprinkle with cheese and walnuts, drizzle with remaining dressing and serve.

Serves 2

roast tomatoes on welsh rarebit

4 vines of cherry tomatoes
   (about 6 tomatoes on each)
20ml olive oil
50g unsalted butter
20g plain flour
80ml beer
20g dry mustard powder
225g strong Cheddar
   cheese, grated
1 egg yolk
4 thick slices rustic bread
chives, cut into 5cm pieces,
   to garnish

Preheat the oven to 220°C/425°F/gas mark 7.

Place the tomatoes on a baking tray, drizzle with olive oil and season with sea salt and pepper. Roast them in the oven for 15 minutes, then set aside and keep warm.

Melt the butter in a saucepan, then add the flour and cook over a low heat, stirring, for 1 minute. Add the beer, mustard and cheese; stir until creamy, but don't allow it to boil. Remove from the heat, add the egg yolk and stir until well combined. Toast the bread slices, evenly spread with the cheese mixture, and place under a grill until hot and bubbling. Top with the tomatoes and garnish with chives.

Serves 4

broad bean bruschetta

4 thick slices rustic bread
40ml extra virgin olive oil,
 plus extra to drizzle
1 garlic clove
250g broad beans, podded
6 radishes, sliced
2 heaped tbsp chopped
 walnuts, toasted
about 20 fresh sage leaves
4 slices prosciutto
50g pecorino pepato cheese*,
 shaved

Preheat the oven to 170°C/325°F/gas mark 3.

Brush the bread with a little of the olive oil, bake for
10 minutes, until golden, then remove and rub with the
garlic clove while still warm.

Meanwhile, place the broad beans in a saucepan of boiling,
salted water and cook for 5 minutes over a high heat. Drain the
beans, refresh under cold water, then, when cool enough to
handle, remove and discard the outer shells. Place the beans
in a bowl along with the radishes, walnuts, sage and remaining
olive oil. Season with salt and pepper.

Place a slice of prosciutto on each bread slice and top with
some of the broad-bean mixture. Garnish with the shaved
cheese, drizzle with extra olive oil and sprinkle with freshly
ground black pepper.

* Pecorino pepato is a sharp, aged sheep's milk cheese embedded with
peppercorns. It is available from good Italian delis.

Serves 4

steak sandwich

20g unsalted butter
2 tsp olive oil
1 onion, sliced into rings
2 x 5mm-thick fillet steaks (125g each)
4 thick slices rye or sourdough bread
50g wild rocket leaves
2 tbsp good-quality tomato chutney

Heat the butter and oil in a large frying pan over a high heat. Add the onions and fry for 3–4 minutes, until lightly browned, then push them to one side of the pan. Add the steaks, season with salt and pepper and cook for 1–2 minutes on each side, until browned but still pink in the centre.

Remove from the heat and allow to rest for 1 minute. Meanwhile, toast the bread. Divide the onion rings between two slices of toast, followed by the steaks. Top with the rocket and tomato chutney, finish with the remaining toast and serve immediately.

Serves 2

crostini with **tuna, lemon & capers**

½ long, thin, rustic loaf, thickly
   sliced on the diagonal
60ml olive oil, plus extra
   for drizzling
2 garlic cloves
125g pitted black olives,
   cut into slivers
1 tbsp salted capers, rinsed
8 semi-dried tomatoes, chopped
1 heaped tbsp chopped
   fresh oregano
125g can smoked tuna
   slices, drained
50g wild rocket

Preheat the oven to 180°C/350°F/gas mark 4.

Brush the bread slices with 20ml of the oil. Place on a baking sheet and bake for 8–10 minutes (or toast on a hot griddle). Halve a garlic clove and rub the cut side over the bread while it is still hot.

Finely chop the remaining garlic and place in a bowl with the olives, capers, tomatoes and oregano. Add the tuna, breaking it up if too large. Place a few rocket leaves on each bread slice, pile on the topping and drizzle with oil.

Serves 3–4

5 nights a week
low-fat

poached chicken with pesto

1 litre chicken stock
250ml dry white wine
1 bay leaf
2 thyme sprigs
1 strip pared lemon rind
2 baby fennel bulbs, trimmed, quartered
4 x 170g skinless chicken breast fillets
8 baby carrots, trimmed
2 small parsnips, peeled, quartered
150g baby green beans, topped
5 tbsp good-quality basil pesto
toasted baguette slices, to serve

Place the stock in a large, deep frying pan with the wine, bay leaf, thyme, lemon rind and fennel. Bring to the boil, then simmer for 3 minutes. Remove the fennel and set aside.

Add the chicken to the stock and poach, uncovered, over a medium-low heat for 15 minutes, or until cooked through. Transfer to a plate and cover loosely with foil to keep warm. Add the carrots and parsnips to the stock and simmer for 5 minutes. Add the beans and cook for a further minute. Return the fennel to the stock to warm through. Season well.

Divide the vegetables among serving bowls and spoon over a little stock. Top with chicken breasts and a dollop of pesto. Season with freshly ground black pepper and serve with toasted slices of bread.

Serves 4

fish baked in a bag with fennel, tomato & cannellini beans

2 x 400g cans cannellini beans, rinsed, drained
200g grape or cherry tomatoes, halved
2 baby fennel, trimmed, thinly sliced, fronds reserved
40ml red wine vinegar
20ml olive oil
4 x 180g skinless firm white fish fillets (such as John Dory, haddock or sea bass)
chopped flat-leaf parsley and lemon wedges, to serve

Preheat the oven to 200°C/400°F/gas mark 6.

Combine the cannellini beans, tomato, fennel, vinegar, oil and 20ml water in a bowl.

Lay out four 30cm sheets of baking paper. Place a fish fillet in the centre of one sheet, top with the bean mixture and season with salt and pepper. Bring the long sides of the paper up to meet in the middle, then fold several times to secure. Twist both ends and tuck under to form a parcel. Repeat with the remaining fish fillets, then place on a tray and bake for 15–20 minutes, until fish is cooked.

Open the parcels and slide the fish and bean mixture onto plates with their juices. Top with the reserved fennel fronds and the parsley, and serve with a lemon wedge.

Serves 4

chicken tenderloins with baby beetroot & ricotta salad

12 (about 90g each)
  chicken tenderloins
60ml olive oil
2 heaped tbsp shredded
  basil leaves
8 canned baby beetroot, drained,
  halved
½ small red onion, thinly sliced
80g baby rocket leaves
2 anchovy fillets,
  roughly chopped
20ml red wine vinegar
60g fresh low-fat ricotta

Combine the chicken, 40ml olive oil and basil in a bowl and season with salt and pepper. Heat a large non-stick frying pan over a high heat and cook the chicken for 2 minutes on each side, or until it is golden and cooked through.

Combine the beetroot, onion, rocket, anchovies, vinegar and remaining oil in a large bowl. Divide the mixture among serving plates and dot with teaspoons of the ricotta. Serve topped with the chicken pieces.

Serves 4

salmon spaghetti
with herbed **sour cream**

230ml extra-light sour cream
5 tbsp chopped mixed herbs
(such as flat-leaf parsley,
chives, basil and dill)
400g spaghetti
20ml olive oil
1 onion, finely chopped
200ml dry white wine
zest of 1 large lemon, plus juice
and extra zest to serve
2 x 175g hot-smoked salmon
fillets*, skin discarded, flaked
into large chunks
small basil sprigs and lemon
juice, to serve

Combine 40ml of the sour cream with 2 teaspoons of the
chopped herbs. Season, then refrigerate the mixture until
ready to serve.

Cook the pasta in a large saucepan of boiling salted water
according to packet instructions.

Meanwhile, heat the oil in a large, deep frying pan over a
medium heat. Add the onion with a pinch of salt and cook
for 3 minutes, or until softened. Add the wine and simmer for
4 minutes, or until reduced by half. Add the lemon zest and
remaining sour cream and cook for 3 minutes, or until slightly
thickened. Season with salt and pepper. Drain the pasta, then
return to the saucepan and toss with the sauce, followed by
the salmon and remaining herbs.

Divide among bowls and top with the herbed sour cream.
Finish with basil sprigs, extra zest and a squeeze of lemon.

* Available from selected supermarkets.

Serves 4

lemon & oregano lamb with cucumber & yoghurt salad

600g (about 8) lean lamb fillets
finely grated rind and juice of ½ a small
   lemon, plus extra wedges to serve
2 heaped tbsp roughly chopped
   oregano leaves
1 tsp honey
2 tsp olive oil

cucumber & yoghurt salad
1 bunch asparagus, cut into 4cm lengths
2 cucumbers, coarsely grated,
   squeezed of excess moisture
1 garlic clove, crushed
200g low-fat natural yoghurt
2 tsp lemon juice
½ tsp ground cumin

Combine the lamb, lemon rind and juice, oregano, honey and olive oil in a bowl. Season with salt and pepper.

For the salad, blanch the asparagus in boiling water for 1 minute. Drain and refresh in cold water, then combine in a bowl with the remaining ingredients. Season to taste with salt and pepper.

Heat a lightly oiled griddle pan over a high heat until just smoking. Add the lamb fillets (in batches if necessary) and cook for 3 minutes each side for medium, or until cooked to your liking.

Remove the fillets from the pan, cover with foil and rest for 4 minutes. Slice the lamb thinly and serve with the salad and lemon wedges.

Serves 4

5 nights a week
kids' favourites

pizza **pie**

28cm-square ready-rolled sheet
   shortcrust pastry
60ml olive oil
2–3 large (400g) onions, thinly sliced
2 garlic cloves, crushed
2 x 400g cans diced tomatoes
1 heaped tbsp chopped fresh
   oregano or basil
50g sliced pepperoni,
   roughly chopped
100g mozzarella cheese, grated
50g anchovy fillets, drained
12 small black olives

Use the pastry sheet to line a 23cm loose-bottomed tart pan. Chill for 30 minutes.

Preheat the oven to 190°C/375°F/gas mark 5.

Line the pastry with non-stick baking paper and fill with rice or pastry weights. Bake for 10 minutes. Remove the paper and weights and return to the oven for 5 minutes, until dry and crisp.

Heat the oil in a large pan. Add the onions and cook over a low heat for 10 minutes, until soft. Add the garlic and cook for 1 minute. Set aside on paper towels for 10 minutes to cool. Strain the tomatoes through a sieve, discarding the juice, then combine with the herbs and season well. Spread the onions on the pastry and top with a layer of pepperoni, then the tomato and half the cheese. Top with the anchovies and olives. Scatter over remaining cheese and bake for 25 minutes, until the cheese has melted.

Serves 6 junior appetites

cheesy **tomato** risotto

30g unsalted butter, plus extra
 to grease
1 litre chicken stock
2 heaped tbsp sun-dried
 tomato paste
40ml olive oil
1 small onion, finely chopped
1 garlic clove, crushed
250g arborio rice
6 slices ham, diced
80g frozen peas
a little unsalted butter, to dot
50g grated Cheddar cheese

Grease a shallow, ovenproof dish with the extra butter.
Place the chicken stock and tomato paste in a small saucepan
and whisk to combine, then simmer gently over a low heat.

Heat the oil in a large pan, then add the onion and garlic.
Cook over a low heat until the onion has softened.

Add the rice and stir for 1 minute to coat the grains of rice
in oil. Add the stock to the rice a ladleful at a time, stirring
occasionally, waiting for all the stock to be absorbed before
adding the next ladle. When all the stock has been absorbed,
season well with salt and pepper.

Stir in the ham and peas, then put the risotto in the dish and
sprinkle with cheese. When ready to serve, dot with butter,
then place under a hot grill until the cheese has melted.

Serves 4 junior appetites or 2 hungry adults

fish pie

200g boneless white fish fillets
  (such as John Dory or haddock)
200g skinless salmon fillet, pin-boned
  (ask your fishmonger to do this)
450ml milk
750g potatoes (such as desiree),
  peeled, chopped
100g unsalted butter
50g flour
150g frozen peas
1 heaped tbsp chopped flat-leaf
  parsley leaves
3 hard-boiled eggs, chopped
juice of ½ lemon
50g grated Cheddar cheese

Preheat the oven to 170°C/325°F/gas mark 3.

Place the fish in a baking dish and season. Pour over 400ml milk, cover with foil and bake for 15 minutes, until the fish flakes away slightly when pressed with a fork. Remove the fish, reserving the milk. When it is cool enough to handle, flake the fish into bite-sized pieces.

Cook the potatoes in boiling salted water until tender. Drain and keep warm. Melt half the butter in a saucepan, stir in the flour and cook over a low heat for 2–3 minutes. Slowly add the reserved milk. Cook until thickened. Add the fish, peas, parsley, egg, lemon juice, salt and pepper.

Mash the potato with the remaining milk and butter, then season. Pile the fish mixture into a 1-litre-capacity baking dish, spoon the mash on top and smooth with a spatula. Trace a pattern into the mash with a fork. Sprinkle with grated cheese. Bake for 20–25 minutes, until golden.

Serves 4–6 junior appetites

cheesy spaghetti with
bacon & peas

500g spaghetti
120g frozen peas
20ml olive oil
4 rashers of bacon, cut into strips
2 garlic cloves, finely chopped
250g smooth ricotta
300ml single cream
80g grated Parmesan, plus extra
　　shaved Parmesan to serve
2 heaped tbsp chopped flat-leaf
　　parsley

Cook the spaghetti in a large saucepan of boiling salted water according to the packet instructions. Add the peas to the pasta for the last 2 minutes of cooking time, then drain both well and return to the saucepan.

Meanwhile, heat the oil in a deep frying pan over a medium heat, add the bacon and cook, stirring, until it starts to crisp. Add the garlic and stir for 30 seconds. Drain off some of the fat. Add the ricotta and cream to the bacon mixture and stir over a low heat until combined and warmed through. Remove from the heat and add to the pasta with the grated Parmesan and parsley. Toss to combine and season to taste.

Serve with extra shaved Parmesan and extra black pepper.

Serves 4 junior appetites

chicken dippers

120g cornflakes
40g plain flour
2 egg whites, lightly beaten
500g skinless chicken breast fillets,
    cut into 3cm pieces
olive-oil spray
green salad, to serve

yoghurt dipping sauce
375ml low-fat yoghurt
½ carrot, grated
½ cucumber, grated
2 garlic cloves, crushed
20ml lemon juice

Preheat the oven to 180°C/350°F/gas mark 4.

Place the cornflakes in a food processor and process until fine crumbs form. Place the cornflake crumbs, flour and egg whites in separate shallow dishes. Dip each chicken piece in the flour to coat lightly, then dip in the egg white and finally in the cornflake crumbs. Place the chicken on a baking tray and spray lightly with oil. Bake in the oven for 10 minutes, then turn the chicken over and return to the oven for 10 minutes more, or until golden brown.

Meanwhile, to make the yoghurt dipping sauce, place all the ingredients in a bowl, season with salt and pepper and stir to combine. Serve the chicken dippers with the dipping sauce and a green salad.

Serves 4 junior appetites

5 nights a week
eggs

leek & mushroom frittata

20g unsalted butter, plus extra
    to grease
20ml olive oil
1 leek (white part only), thinly sliced
400g button or mixed mushrooms,
    washed, sliced
2 garlic cloves, crushed
8 eggs
150ml double cream
40g grated Parmesan
3 heaped tbsp torn basil leaves
tomato relish, to serve

Preheat the oven to 180°C/350°F/gas mark 4. Lightly grease a 20cm-square cake pan with the extra butter.

Melt the butter with the oil in a large frying pan over a medium-low heat. Add the leek and cook for 5 minutes, until soft but not browned. Add the mushrooms and garlic and cook, stirring, for 5 minutes, or until the mushrooms are soft.

Meanwhile, whisk the eggs, cream and Parmesan in a jug. Season with salt and pepper. Fill the prepared pan with the leek mixture, sprinkle with basil and pour over the egg mixture. Bake for 25–30 minutes, until lightly browned and set. Cool slightly, then turn out onto a board. Cut into squares and serve with the tomato relish.

Serves 4

soft tacos

2 vine-ripened tomatoes,
  seeds removed, finely chopped
1 red chilli, seeds removed,
  finely chopped
3 heaped tbsp sliced
  coriander leaves
20ml olive oil
4–6 drops Tabasco
  sauce (optional)
4 flour tortillas
8 eggs, lightly beaten
60ml single cream

Combine the tomato, chilli, half the coriander and 2 teaspoons of oil. Add drops of Tabasco if desired, and season to taste.

Wrap the stacked tortillas in paper towels, place them on a plate and microwave on high for 1 minute. Turn the stack and heat for a further 30 seconds. Or heat in the oven according to the packet directions.

Lightly whisk eggs with cream and remaining coriander. Season with salt and pepper. Heat the remaining oil in a large pan over a medium-high heat, pour in the eggs and, using a wooden spoon, fold for 2 minutes until scrambled and almost set. Remove from the heat. Working with one tortilla at a time (keep the rest covered as you work), spoon some egg down the centre, top with salsa and fold over the sides to enclose. Secure with a paper napkin if desired, and serve with any remaining salsa on the side.

Makes 4

fragrant egg curry

1 Spanish onion, chopped
40g grated fresh ginger
2 garlic cloves, crushed
40ml light olive oil
40g good-quality curry powder
½ tsp ground turmeric
1 cinnamon stick
10 fresh curry leaves*
425g can diced tomatoes
8 hard-boiled eggs
70g red lentils
120g frozen peas
2 heaped tbsp chopped
   coriander
cooked rice, to serve

Place the onion, ginger and garlic in a food processor and process to form a paste.

Heat the oil in a heavy-based saucepan, add the paste and cook over a low heat for 2–3 minutes. Add the spices and cook for 1 minute, stirring to release the flavours. Add the tomatoes and 500ml water and bring to the boil. Reduce the heat to medium and simmer for 15 minutes.

Meanwhile, shell and halve the eggs and add to the pan with the lentils and peas – if the mixture is too thick, add an extra 125ml water. Cook over a low heat for 15 minutes, or until the lentils are soft. Stir in the coriander and serve with the cooked rice.

* Available from selected greengrocers and Asian food shops.

Serves 4

coriander & sweetcorn omelette rolls

4 eggs
125g can sweetcorn kernels,
    rinsed and drained
20ml light soy sauce
20ml vegetable oil
1 heaped tbsp Thai green
    curry paste
6 spring onions, thinly sliced
1 red chilli, seeds removed,
    chopped
120g coriander leaves,
    plus extra to garnish
sweet chilli sauce, to serve

Place the eggs, sweetcorn and soy in a bowl with 40ml of
water, beat to combine, then set aside.

Heat half of the oil in a small non-stick frying pan over a
medium-low heat. Add half the egg mixture to cover the base
of the pan, then cook until set. Carefully remove from the pan
and keep warm. Repeat with the remaining mixture.

Place the omelettes on a clean chopping board and spread half
the green curry paste over each. Sprinkle the spring onion and
chilli over the top, reserving a little of each for garnish,
followed by the coriander. Roll up each omelette tightly, then
cut in half on the diagonal.

Place each omelette on a serving plate, garnish with the
remaining spring onion and chilli, plus extra coriander
and serve with the sweet chilli sauce.

Serves 2

moroccan eggs

20ml olive oil, plus extra to drizzle
4 eggs
2 heaped tbsp dukkah*
4 slices Turkish bread, split, toasted
130g hummus
½ red onion, sliced
5 tbsp mint leaves
tomato chutney, to serve

Heat the oil in a large non-stick frying pan over a medium-high heat. Crack the eggs into the pan and cook for about 30 seconds, until the whites start to firm, then sprinkle the dukkah over each egg. Cover loosely and cook the eggs for another minute for runny yolks, or to your liking.

Meanwhile, thickly spread the toast with hummus and place on warm plates. Top with the eggs, drizzle with a little extra oil and scatter over the sliced onion and mint leaves. Serve topped with chutney.

* Dukkah is an Egyptian spice, nut and seed blend, available from Middle Eastern and gourmet food shops.

Serves 4

5 nights a week
peas & beans

spaghetti bean bolognese

40ml olive oil
1 onion, finely chopped
1 carrot, chopped
1 celery stalk, chopped
2 garlic cloves, crushed
2 heaped tbsp tomato paste
250ml red wine
1 tsp chopped rosemary
1 bay leaf
700ml passata (sugo)
250ml vegetable stock
2 x 400g cans four-bean mix,
    drained, rinsed
1 heaped tbsp chopped flat-leaf
    parsley
500g spaghetti
shaved Parmesan, to serve

Heat the oil in a large saucepan over a low heat, add the onion, carrot and celery and cook for about 10 minutes, stirring occasionally, until softened. Add the garlic and tomato paste and cook, stirring, for 2 minutes, then increase the heat to medium, add the wine and allow to bubble for 2–3 minutes. Add the rosemary, bay leaf, passata and stock, reduce the heat to low and cook for 10 minutes. Add the beans and cook for a further 5 minutes, adding more stock or water if the sauce is too thick. Stir through the parsley and season.

Meanwhile, cook the spaghetti in a large pan of boiling salted water according to the packet instructions. Drain, toss through sauce and serve with shaved Parmesan.

Serves 6

pea risotto with prawns

80ml extra virgin olive oil
1 tsp lemon zest
30ml lemon juice
4 garlic cloves
500g raw prawns, peeled,
  tails intact
8 spring onions, roughly chopped
100g baby spinach leaves
40g flat-leaf parsley
2 heaped tbsp fresh tarragon leaves
300g arborio rice
150ml dry white wine
1.5 litres vegetable stock
300g frozen peas
50g unsalted butter
80g grated Parmesan, plus extra
  to serve

Combine 20ml oil, the lemon zest and juice in a bowl with 1 crushed garlic clove. Season, toss the prawns in the marinade, then refrigerate while you make the risotto. Whiz the spring onion, spinach, parsley, tarragon and the remaining garlic to a coarse paste in a food processor and set aside.

Heat the remaining oil in a deep frying pan over a medium heat. Add the rice and stir for 2 minutes. Add the wine and stir until absorbed. Add the stock a ladleful at a time, allowing each to be absorbed before adding the next. Continue, stirring, for 15–20 minutes, until you have one ladleful of stock left and the rice is cooked but still firm to the bite. With the last ladle of stock, add the peas and spinach mix. Once all the stock is added, cook for 1 minute, then add the butter and cheese. Remove from the heat and cover to keep warm.

Heat a non-stick pan over a medium heat. Add the prawns and marinade and cook, stirring, for 3–4 minutes, until they are opaque. Divide the risotto and prawns among bowls and serve with extra Parmesan.

Serves 4

split pea, watercress & goat's curd salad

200g green split peas
20ml olive oil
juice of 1 lemon
2 tsp ground coriander
½ tsp ground ginger
1 red onion, very finely chopped
1 bunch watercress, stalks trimmed
2 roasted red peppers*, cut into strips
50g goat's curd*

Cook the peas in a saucepan of boiling salted water for 15–18 minutes, until tender but firm to the bite.

Meanwhile, place the oil, lemon juice, spices and onion in a large bowl and whisk until combined. Drain the peas well and add to the dressing. Season to taste and toss to combine. Stand for 10 minutes, then toss with the watercress and roasted pepper. Divide among plates and top with goat's curd.

* Roasted pepper is available from delis and selected supermarkets. Goat's curd is available from delis and gourmet food shops; substitute soft goat's cheese.

Serves 4

roast chicken with peas & bacon

20ml vegetable oil
15g unsalted butter
2 chicken breast fillets, skin on
1 onion, finely chopped
4 bacon rashers, rind removed, chopped
20g plain flour
150ml chicken stock
juice of 1 orange
100g frozen peas, thawed
2 heaped tbsp chopped flat-leaf parsley
mashed parsnip, to serve

Preheat the oven to 200°C/400°F/gas mark 6.

Heat the oil and butter in a large frying pan over a medium heat, add the chicken skin-side down and cook for 2–3 minutes, until golden. Transfer to a baking tray (skin-side up) and roast for 10–15 minutes.

Meanwhile, return the pan to the heat, add the onion and fry for 1 minute. Add the bacon and fry for 2 minutes, until the onion is golden and the bacon is crisp. Add the flour and cook, stirring, for 1 minute. Add the stock and orange juice and cook, stirring, for 1–2 minutes, until thickened.

Season, add the peas and heat for a further minute, then stir through the parsley. Return the chicken to the pan to coat in the sauce. Serve on mashed parsnip. Spoon over any remaining sauce.

Serves 2

four-bean soup with barley

20ml olive oil
1 onion, roughly chopped
3 garlic cloves, sliced
1 celery stalk, roughly chopped
1 carrot, roughly chopped
3 thyme sprigs
105g pearl barley
500ml salt-reduced
  vegetable stock
2 x 400g cans four-bean mix,
  rinsed, drained
400g can chopped tomatoes
30g thinly sliced flat-leaf
  parsley leaves

Heat the oil in a large, deep saucepan over a low heat. Add the chopped onion, garlic, celery, carrot and thyme, and cook, stirring, for 8–10 minutes, until the onion is soft. Add the barley and stir to coat in the onion mixture. Add the vegetable stock and 1 litre water, then bring to the boil. Reduce the heat to medium-low and simmer for 20 minutes, or until the barley is slightly tender.

Add the beans and tomato and stir to combine. Bring back to a simmer and cook for a further 15 minutes, or until the barley is soft. Serve in bowls sprinkled with parsley.

Serves 4

5 nights a week
vegetarian

spicy bean & **chilli fajitas**

40ml olive oil
1 onion, finely chopped
2 garlic cloves, crushed
1 red pepper, chopped
1 small red chilli, seeds removed,
  finely chopped
2 tsp ground cumin
190g jar sun-dried tomato pesto
2 x 400g cans red kidney beans,
  rinsed, drained
425g can chopped tomatoes
1 tsp caster sugar
warmed flour tortillas, guacamole,
  lettuce, sour cream, coriander
  leaves and grated Cheddar,
  to serve

In a large, heavy-based saucepan, heat the oil over a low heat. Add the onion and cook for 5 minutes, until soft. Add the garlic, red pepper and chilli and cook, stirring, for a further minute. Add the cumin, pesto, beans, tomatoes and sugar. Cook over a low heat for 15 minutes, until slightly reduced, stirring occasionally. Season.

Serve with tortillas for wrapping, with the guacamole, lettuce leaves, sour cream, coriander and grated cheese.

Serves 4

lentil & vegetable cottage pie

20ml vegetable oil
1 onion, finely chopped
2 celery stalks, chopped
1 large carrot, chopped
2 garlic cloves, crushed
2 heaped tbsp sun-dried
  tomato pesto
260g tomato passata (sugo)
1 bay leaf
1 heaped tbsp chopped thyme
250ml vegetable stock
400g can lentils, rinsed, drained
800g potatoes, peeled, chopped
100g unsalted butter
125ml milk
2 egg yolks
100g grated Cheddar*

Preheat the oven to 200°C/400°F/gas mark 6.

In a large pan, heat the oil over a medium heat and cook the onion for 1–2 minutes. Add the celery, carrot and garlic and cook for 1 minute. Add the pesto, passata, bay leaf, thyme and stock. Simmer gently for 15 minutes, until the vegetables are cooked. Stir in the lentils, season, then transfer to a 1.2-litre baking dish.

Meanwhile, cook the potatoes in boiling salted water until tender. Drain and mash. Stir in the butter, milk, yolks and cheese. Spread over the lentil mixture and roughen the top with a fork. Bake for 15 minutes, or until bubbling and golden.

* Look for animal rennet-free (vegetarian) cheddar, available from selected supermarkets.

Serves 3–4

vegetable tagine

40ml olive oil
1 onion, chopped
2 garlic cloves, crushed
1 heaped tbsp grated ginger
2 tsp ground cumin
2 tsp ground coriander
1 tsp paprika
1 cinnamon stick
1kg pumpkin, peeled, cut into
   2.5cm cubes
400g can chopped tomatoes
500ml vegetable stock
175g thin green beans, topped
2 heaped tbsp chopped mint
2 heaped tbsp chopped coriander
40ml honey
couscous, tossed with drained
   canned chickpeas and
   chopped red onion, to serve

Heat the olive oil in a large, deep frying pan over a medium heat. Cook the onion for 3–4 minutes, or until softened. Add the crushed garlic and grated ginger to the pan and cook, stirring, for 30 seconds, until fragrant. Add the ground cumin, coriander, paprika and cinnamon stick, then stir for a further minute until fragrant. Add the cubed pumpkin, canned tomatoes and the vegetable stock, and stir to combine. Season to taste with sea salt and freshly ground black pepper. Bring to the boil, then reduce the heat to medium-low and simmer the tagine for 12–15 minutes, uncovered, until the pumpkin is tender.

Add the green beans and cook for a further 5 minutes, until they are tender and bright green. When you are ready to serve, stir in the chopped mint, coriander and honey. Serve in bowls with the couscous.

Serves 4

cottage cheese pancakes with roasted pepper salsa

120g plain flour
¾ tsp baking powder
¼ tsp bicarbonate of soda
200g low-fat cottage cheese,
   plus extra to serve
2 egg whites

roasted pepper salsa
40ml olive oil
1 small red onion, chopped
2 roasted red peppers*, diced
40ml balsamic vinegar
3 tbsp basil leaves, chopped,
   plus extra torn basil to garnish

For the salsa, heat half the oil in a frying pan over a medium-low heat. Add the onion and pepper and cook for 5 minutes, until the onion is softened. Add the balsamic vinegar and basil, and season. Warm through for 1–2 minutes, then set aside.

For the pancakes, sift the flour, baking powder and soda into a bowl. Stir in the cottage cheese and season.

In a separate bowl, whisk the egg whites until soft peaks form, then carefully fold into the cottage cheese mixture. Heat the remaining olive oil in a non-stick frying pan over a medium heat. Place tablespoonfuls of batter into the pan and cook for 1 minute each side, until golden, then remove and keep warm. Continue with the remaining mixture. Serve with salsa and extra cottage cheese. Garnish with basil.

* Roasted pepper is available from delis and selected supermarkets.

Makes 12

vegetable **samosa** pies

500g potatoes, peeled, cut into
  1cm cubes
350g sweet potato (kumara),
  peeled, cut into 1cm cubes
20ml vegetable oil
1 large onion, chopped
1 tsp cumin seeds
½ tsp ground ginger
2 tsp mild curry powder
2 garlic cloves, crushed
120g frozen peas
400g can chopped tomatoes,
  drained of excess liquid
2 heaped tbsp chopped
  coriander leaves
1 egg, beaten
20ml lemon juice
8 sheets filo pastry
80g unsalted butter, melted
2 tbsp sesame seeds
mango chutney, to serve

Preheat the oven to 180°C/350°F/gas mark 4. Place a baking sheet in the oven to heat (this will give the pies a crisp base). Grease six individual pie dishes.

Cook the potato and sweet potato in boiling salted water until tender, then drain well and set aside. Heat the oil in a deep frying pan over a medium heat, add the onion and cook, stirring, for 2 minutes, or until soft. Add the cumin seeds, ground ginger and curry powder and stir for 1 minute, or until fragrant. Add the garlic, peas, tomatoes, potato and sweet potato and cook, stirring, for 2 minutes. Stir in the coriander, then remove from the heat and set aside to cool. Stir the egg and lemon juice into the cooled mixture and season to taste.

Place the pastry on a work surface and cover with a damp tea towel. Lay out one sheet and brush with melted butter, then place another sheet of pastry on top, repeating until you have four layers. Use scissors to cut into six 14cm squares and use to line the dishes, leaving some overhanging. Fill the pastry with the vegetable mixture.

Place another sheet of filo on the work surface, then place another sheet of pastry on top, repeating with the remaining pastry. Using scissors or a round pastry cutter, cut six 14cm-diameter circles and place on top of each pie. Fold the excess pastry over the lids and pinch to secure. Brush the tops with remaining butter and sprinkle with sesame seeds. Place the pies on the preheated tray and bake for 20 minutes, or until golden. Serve warm with mango chutney.

Makes 6

5 nights a week
stir-fry

beef mince with
french beans

300g beef mince
1 tsp chicken stock powder
1 tsp cornflour
20ml vegetable oil
2 garlic cloves, finely chopped
600g French beans, trimmed,
   cut into 3cm lengths
½ onion, peeled, finely chopped
1 tsp finely chopped ginger
1 tsp oyster sauce
1 tsp light soy sauce
steamed rice, to serve

Place the beef in a small bowl with the stock and cornflour and use a fork to combine. Set aside. Heat half the oil in a wok over a high heat, add half the garlic and stir-fry until fragrant. Add the beans and stir-fry for 1–2 minutes, until cooked through. Remove from the wok and set aside.

Heat the remaining oil in the wok, add the remaining garlic, the onion and ginger. Stir-fry over a high heat until fragrant. Add the mince and cook for 2–3 minutes, until browned. Add the sauces and cook for 1–2 minutes. Return the beans to the wok and cook for 1 minute.
Serve with steamed rice.

Serves 4

pork satay noodles

250g dried egg noodles
1 tsp sesame oil
20ml peanut oil
500g pork mince
1 small onion, roughly chopped
1 small red chilli, seeds removed,
  finely chopped
2 heaped tbsp good-quality satay paste
40ml fish sauce
40ml kecap manis*
4 tbsp crushed unsalted peanuts
200ml coconut milk
2 kaffir lime leaves*, thinly shredded
2 heaped tbsp chopped fresh coriander
lime wedges, to serve

Cook the noodles in boiling salted water according to the packet directions. Drain and toss with the sesame oil.

Heat the peanut oil in a wok over a high heat. When hot, add the pork and onion and stir-fry for 2–3 minutes, until cooked through. Add the chilli and satay paste and stir-fry for a few seconds, then add the fish sauce, kecap manis, peanuts, coconut milk and lime leaves. Cook for a further 2–3 minutes, then toss through the noodles and coriander. Serve in bowls with lime wedges.

* Kecap manis is available from Asian and selected supermarkets. Kaffir lime leaves are from selected greengrocers and Asian food shops.

Serves 4

spicy tofu stir-fry

20ml vegetable oil
2 garlic cloves, crushed
150g small fresh shiitake mushrooms
  (or large shiitakes, roughly chopped)
200g spicy tofu*, sliced
6 spring onions, cut into 3cm lengths
1 red pepper, seeds removed,
  cut into thin strips
150g mange-tout, trimmed
40ml soy sauce
40ml kecap manis*
cooked rice, to serve
coriander leaves, to garnish

Heat the oil in a wok over a high heat, add the garlic and stir-fry for 30 seconds. Add the mushrooms and tofu and stir-fry for 1 minute. Add the spring onions, red pepper and mange-tout, stir-fry for a further 1–2 minutes, then stir in the soy sauce and kecap manis. Serve with rice and garnish with coriander.

* Spicy tofu is available from supermarkets and health food shops. Kecap manis is available from Asian and selected supermarkets.

Serves 4

chicken & **peanut** stir-fry

500g chicken thigh fillets,
    cut into 1cm cubes
1 heaped tbsp caster sugar
40ml hoisin sauce
40ml soy sauce
20ml peanut oil
1 green pepper, chopped
1 small onion, chopped
227g canned sliced water
    chestnuts, drained
40ml Chinese rice wine*
75g peanuts, roasted
steamed rice, to serve
80g coriander leaves

Toss the chicken in the sugar and half of each of hoisin and soy. Heat half the oil in a non-stick wok over a high heat. Drain half the chicken and stir-fry for 5 minutes, or until cooked through. Remove from the pan with a slotted spoon. Repeat with the remaining oil and chicken.

Reduce the heat to medium and add the green pepper, onion and remaining hoisin and soy. Stir-fry for 5 minutes, or until tender. Return the chicken to the wok, add the water chestnuts and rice wine. Simmer until the wine is reduced by half. Remove from the heat and add the peanuts. Serve on the rice and garnish with the coriander.

* Chinese rice wine (shaohsing) is available from Asian supermarkets. Substitute dry sherry.

Serves 4

five-spice vegetable stir-fry

1½ tsp cornflour
40ml light soy sauce
40ml Chinese rice wine*
1 tsp caster sugar
2 tsp five-spice powder
20ml vegetable oil
2 red peppers, thinly sliced
1 yellow pepper, thinly sliced
2 bunches tenderstem broccoli,
   trimmed, halved on the diagonal
200g fresh shiitake mushrooms,
   thinly sliced
steamed medium-grain white rice,
   to serve

Combine the cornflour and 80ml cold water in a bowl. Add the soy sauce, Chinese rice wine, sugar and five-spice, and mix well.

Meanwhile, heat the oil in a wok over a high heat until smoking. Add the vegetables and stir-fry for 2 minutes. Add the sauce mixture and stir-fry for 2 minutes, or until the vegetables have softened but are still crunchy, and the sauce has thickened. Divide the stir-fry among serving plates and serve with steamed rice.

* Chinese rice wine (shaohsing) is available from Asian supermarkets. Substitute dry sherry.

Serves 4

5 nights a week
risotto

avocado & prawn risotto

1.25 litres vegetable stock
25g unsalted butter
20ml olive oil
1 onion, finely chopped
3 garlic cloves, crushed
400g arborio rice
165ml dry white wine
500g prawns, roughly chopped
80g grated Parmesan,
   plus extra to serve
2 avocados
juice of 1 lemon
3 tbsp roughly chopped chives

Place the stock in a saucepan, bring to the boil, then reduce the heat to low and keep the stock at a simmer.

Meanwhile, heat the butter and olive oil in a deep frying pan over a medium heat, add the onion and cook, stirring, for 1–2 minutes, until softened but not coloured. Stir in the garlic, then add the rice and cook, stirring, for 1 minute to coat the grains. Add the wine and allow the liquid to evaporate. Add the stock, a ladleful at a time, stirring occasionally, allowing each ladleful to be absorbed before adding the next. Continue until you have one ladleful of stock left – this should take about 20 minutes. Add the prawns with the final ladleful of stock and continue to stir for 2–3 minutes until the prawns are cooked through. Stir in the Parmesan, then cover and remove from the heat.

Peel the avocados, dice and toss in the lemon juice. Just before serving, carefully stir the avocado mixture into the risotto. Serve in bowls topped with extra Parmesan and chopped chives.

Serves 4

prawn & lemon risotto

225g sugar snap peas
1 courgette, thickly sliced
2 tbsp olive oil
1 onion, finely chopped
½ tsp saffron threads
250g arborio rice
1 garlic clove, crushed
225g button mushrooms, sliced
juice and grated rind of 1 lemon
750ml fish or vegetable stock
300g cooked prawns, peeled,
   deveined, tails intact
4 tbsp chopped flat-leaf parsley
unsalted butter (optional), to serve

Blanch the sugar snap peas and courgette in boiling water for 1 minute, then drain, refresh under cold water and drain again. Set aside.

Heat the oil in a large frying pan. Add the onion and saffron, and cook over a low heat for 2–3 minutes, or until the onion is softened but not coloured. Add the rice, garlic and mushrooms and cook, stirring, for 2 minutes. Add the lemon rind and a third of the stock and simmer, stirring occasionally, until most of the liquid is absorbed. Repeat twice by separately adding the remaining thirds of stock.

Add the prawns, blanched vegetables and lemon juice, and cook for 1–2 minutes, or until heated through. Stir in parsley, and a little butter if desired, then season and serve.

Serves 4

prosciutto & fontina oven-baked risotto

20g unsalted butter
40ml olive oil
1 large onion, finely chopped
1 garlic clove, crushed
400g arborio rice
1 tsp smoked paprika (pimentón)*
125ml dry sherry
1 litre hot chicken stock
3 sprigs thyme, plus 1 tbsp
    thyme leaves
2 bunches asparagus,
    ends trimmed
100g prosciutto, thinly sliced
35g grated fontina cheese*

Preheat the oven to 180°C/350°F/gas mark 4.

Heat the butter and half the oil in a flameproof and oven-proof dish on the hob over a medium-low heat. Add the onion and garlic and cook, stirring, for 5 minutes, or until soft. Add the rice and paprika and stir. Add the sherry, bring to the boil then simmer, uncovered, for 1 minute, until the sherry is absorbed. Add the stock and thyme sprigs. Cover and cook in the oven for 20–25 minutes, or until the liquid is absorbed and the rice is tender. Stir once during cooking.

Toss the asparagus in the remaining oil and spread on a baking tray with the prosciutto. Place in the oven for the last 10 minutes of the rice cooking time to cook the asparagus and crisp the prosciutto. Chop the asparagus finely on the diagonal and break the prosciutto into shards. To serve, stir the asparagus, thyme leaves and cheese through the rice and top with prosciutto.

* Smoked paprika is available from gourmet food shops and delis. Fontina is available from selected delis. Substitute gruyère or gouda.

Serves 4

duck & shiitake risotto

40ml olive oil
1 onion, finely chopped
2 garlic cloves, chopped
150g fresh shiitake mushrooms
350g arborio rice
1.25 litres chicken stock
60ml Chinese rice wine*
40ml kecap manis*
1 tsp sesame oil
1 Chinese barbecued duck*,
   meat roughly chopped
1 bunch baby bok choy

Preheat the oven to 200°C/400°F/gas mark 6.

Heat the oil in a large, deep frying pan over a medium heat and cook the onion and garlic for 1–2 minutes, until softened. Add the mushrooms and rice, and stir for a further minute. Add the stock and wine, bring to the boil, then transfer to a large greased baking dish. Cover with foil and bake for 20–25 minutes. Stir in the kecap manis, sesame oil and duck, cover and rest for 5 minutes, until the liquid is absorbed. Meanwhile, lightly steam then roughly chop the bok choy. Stir into the risotto and serve.

* Chinese rice wine (shaohsing) is available from Asian supermarkets. Substitute dry sherry. Kecap manis is available from Asian and selected supermarkets. Chinese barbecued duck is available from Chinese barbecue shops and restaurants, where you can also buy steamed bok choy.

Serves 4

blt risotto

8 bacon rashers
1 litre vegetable or chicken stock
20ml olive oil, plus extra to drizzle
1 leek (white part only),
   finely chopped
2 garlic cloves, crushed
300g arborio rice
60ml dry white wine
400g vine-ripened cherry tomatoes
80g grated Parmesan, plus extra
   shaved Parmesan, to serve
1 heaped tbsp finely chopped
   flat-leaf parsley
40g unsalted butter, cut into 4 pieces

This isn't your traditional BLT combo; this risotto contains bacon, leek and tomato.

Remove the tail ends of the bacon rashers, roll up and secure with a toothpick. Place in the fridge until needed. Dice the remaining bacon.

Preheat the oven to 200°C/400°F/gas mark 6.

Place the stock in a pan over a medium-high heat and bring to the boil. Reduce the heat to low and simmer.

Heat the oil in a pan over a medium heat. Stir in the leek and diced bacon for 2–3 minutes, or until the leek is soft and the bacon starts to colour. Add the garlic and rice, and stir for 2 minutes. Add the wine and stir until absorbed. Add the stock a ladleful at a time, stirring until absorbed between additions, until the rice is cooked but still firm to the bite (this should take about 15–20 minutes).

Meanwhile, place the tomatoes and bacon curls on a baking tray, drizzle with oil and season the tomatoes. Roast for 10 minutes, or until the tomatoes are just soft and the bacon is crisp. Set a few tomatoes aside. Remove the stalks from the remaining tomatoes and stir into the risotto with the grated Parmesan and parsley, then season. Serve the risotto topped with butter and garnish with the tomatoes, bacon curls and shaved Parmesan.

Serves 4

5 nights a week
pasta

roasted tomato & chilli pasta with parsley salad

250g Roma tomatoes, halved
250g cherry tomatoes
2 garlic cloves
1 long red chilli
100ml extra virgin olive oil
2 roasted red peppers*
½ tsp smoked paprika (pimentón)*
1 tsp caster sugar
20ml red wine vinegar
400g spaghetti
110g flat-leaf parsley leaves
50g shaved Parmesan
20ml lemon juice

Preheat the oven to 170°C/325°F/gas mark 3.

Spread the tomatoes, garlic and chilli on a baking tray, drizzle with 20ml of the oil and season with salt and pepper. Roast for 8 minutes, then remove the cherry tomatoes and reserve to use for a garnish. Roast the remaining tomatoes, garlic and chilli for a further 5 minutes.

Cool slightly, then peel the Roma tomatoes and place in a blender with the garlic and chilli (remove the seeds if you don't want the sauce to be hot). Blend with the red peppers, paprika, sugar and vinegar, then season. With the motor running, slowly pour in 40ml of the oil and blend until combined and smooth.

Cook the pasta in a large pan of boiling salted water according to the packet instructions, then drain. Warm through the sauce in the same pan, then return the pasta to the pan and toss to coat well.

Place the parsley and Parmesan in a bowl with the lemon juice and remaining 40ml oil. Season with salt and pepper and toss gently to combine. Divide the pasta among serving bowls and top with the cherry tomatoes and some of the parsley salad.

* Roasted pepper is available from delis and selected supermarkets. Smoked paprika is available from gourmet food shops and delis.

Serves 4

pumpkin, sage & ricotta lasagne

1.2kg pumpkin, peeled,
  cut into 2cm pieces
40ml olive oil
½ tsp dried chilli flakes
1 heaped tbsp chopped
  sage, plus 12 whole leaves,
  to serve
¼ tsp freshly grated nutmeg
350g ricotta
1 egg
80g grated Parmesan,
  plus extra to serve
8 fresh lasagne sheets
100g unsalted butter
2 heaped tbsp chopped
  walnuts

Preheat the oven to 190°C/375°F/gas mark 5.

Place the pumpkin on a baking tray, drizzle with oil, sprinkle with chilli flakes and season. Cover with foil and roast for 25 minutes, or until the pumpkin is tender. Allow to cool slightly. Purée the pumpkin in a food processor with the chopped sage and nutmeg. Set aside. In a clean processor, process the ricotta, egg, Parmesan, salt and pepper. Lightly grease a 24cm-square baking dish. Lay two lasagne sheets over the base and spread with half the pumpkin. Add another layer of lasagne sheets, then spread with half the ricotta mixture. Repeat this process. Sprinkle the final layer of ricotta with extra Parmesan. Lay a sheet of baking paper over the surface, cover with foil and bake for 35 minutes. Uncover and bake for 15 minutes more, until golden. Stand for 5 minutes.

Meanwhile, heat the butter, sage leaves and walnuts in a pan for 1–2 minutes over a medium heat, until the butter starts to foam. Remove from the heat. Serve the lasagne drizzled with sage butter and scattered with extra Parmesan.

Serves 4

simple all'amatriciana

1 onion, quartered
2 garlic cloves
1 small red chilli, seeds removed
125g piece pancetta, rind
   removed, roughly chopped
40ml olive oil
400g can crushed tomatoes
250ml chicken stock
400g short pasta (such
   as rigatoni)
2 heaped tbsp chopped
   flat-leaf parsley
40g grated Parmesan

Place the onion, garlic, chilli and pancetta in a food processor, and process until the mixture is roughly chopped. Heat the oil in a heavy-based frying pan over a medium-low heat. Cook the pancetta mixture, stirring occasionally, for 5 minutes, or until the onion softens. Add the tomatoes, stock and 80ml water, then bring to the boil. Reduce the heat to low and simmer for 10 minutes, or until the sauce thickens.

Cook the pasta in a large pan of boiling salted water according to the packet instructions. Drain well. Toss the pasta with the sauce, then season well to taste. Stir in the chopped parsley and half of the grated Parmesan and serve sprinkled with the remaining Parmesan.

Serves 4

lemon & basil spaghetti

500g spaghetti
50g unsalted butter
300ml thickened cream
60ml lemon juice
grated zest of 3 lemons
100g grated Parmesan,
    plus extra to serve
½ tsp freshly grated nutmeg
40g basil leaves

Cook the pasta in a large saucepan of boiling salted water according to the packet instructions.

Meanwhile, combine the butter, cream and lemon juice in a small pan and place over a low heat until the butter melts. Remove from the heat.

Drain the pasta, reserving 250ml of the cooking water, then return the pasta to the pan. Add the cream mixture, lemon zest and enough cooking water to allow the sauce to coat. Add the Parmesan and nutmeg, then season to taste. Sprinkle with basil leaves and extra Parmesan to serve.

Serves 4

ravioli with **rocket** & **balsamic** dressing

75g semi-dried tomatoes
80g baby rocket
½ red onion, thinly sliced
1 heaped tbsp salted capers,
   rinsed, drained
2 heaped tbsp basil leaves
50g pitted kalamata olives
400g goat's cheese ravioli
60ml extra virgin olive oil,
   plus extra to toss the pasta
30ml balsamic vinegar
shaved Parmesan, to serve

Place the tomatoes, rocket, sliced onion, capers, basil and olives in a bowl. Set aside

Cook the ravioli in salted boiling water according to packet instructions. Drain and toss in the extra olive oil to keep the pasta separate.

Place the olive oil and vinegar in a screw-top jar, season with salt and pepper and shake well to combine. Add the dressing to the salad mixture with the hot pasta and carefully toss together. Using tongs, pile onto serving plates. Serve topped with some Parmesan shavings.

Serves 2

5 nights a week
pastry

rustic cheese, **egg** & **bacon** pie

375g block frozen puff pastry, thawed
200g crème fraîche or full-fat
    sour cream
180g coarsely grated vintage Cheddar
1 egg, plus 2 egg yolks
2 bacon rashers, chopped
2 tsp fresh thyme leaves
milk, to brush
green salad dressed with olive oil
    and balsamic vinegar, to serve

Preheat the oven to 200°C/400°F/gas mark 6. Line a large baking tray with baking paper.

On a lightly floured surface, roll out the pastry to a 20cm x 30cm rectangle, then lay the pastry on the prepared baking tray.

In a bowl, mix together the crème fraîche, grated cheese, egg and yolks, bacon and thyme, then season with sea salt and freshly ground black pepper.

Spread the egg mixture over the pastry, leaving a 2cm border. Brush the exposed pastry with a little milk, then bake for 15 minutes, or until puffed and golden. Slice the pie and serve with salad.

Serves 4–6

sausage pastry

700g good-quality sausages,
    meat removed from casings
20ml olive oil
1 large onion, chopped
2 garlic cloves, chopped
1 heaped tbsp tomato paste
250ml passata (sugo)
1 heaped tbsp chopped
    flat-leaf parsley
375g block frozen puff
    pastry, thawed
plain flour, to dust
1 egg, beaten
quick chilli sauce
    (see recipe below), to serve

Heat the oil in a saucepan over a medium-low heat, add the onion and garlic, and cook, stirring, for 5 minutes, or until the onion has softened. Increase the heat to high and add the sausage meat. Cook, stirring with a wooden spoon to break it up. When the meat is starting to brown, stir in the tomato paste, passata and 80ml water. Cook for a further 5 minutes. Set aside to cool. Place the mixture in a food processor with the parsley and pulse gently until just combined. Season to taste.

Preheat the oven to 180°C/350°F/gas mark 4. Line a baking tray with baking paper.

Cut the pastry in half lengthways. Roll out one piece on a lightly floured board to a 18cm x 35cm rectangle. Place on the tray and top with the sausage mixture, leaving a 2cm border. Brush the border with water. Roll out the remaining pastry on a lightly floured board so that it is slightly larger than the first rectangle. Make several small slashes across the middle of the pastry. Place over the sausage meat and seal the edges together. Brush the pastry with beaten egg and bake for 25 minutes, until puffed and golden. Serve with the quick chilli sauce.

Serves 4–6

quick chilli sauce

400g can chopped tomatoes
100ml sweet chilli sauce
juice of 1 lime
1 heaped tbsp brown sugar
1 long red chilli, seeds removed,
    chopped

This will keep in the fridge for up to a week.

Combine all the ingredients in a small saucepan. Bring to a simmer over a low heat and cook for 10 minutes, until thickened. Season to taste and cool. Pulse in a food processor to purée.

Serves 4

four-cheese **galette**

150g marinated feta cheese
120g full-fat ricotta cheese
90g mozzarella cheese, grated
4 tbsp grated Parmesan
1 heaped tbsp chopped
 fresh thyme
60ml crème fraîche
1 egg, lightly beaten
5 sheets filo pastry,
 cut into 28cm squares
30g unsalted butter, melted

Preheat the oven to 190°C/375°F/gas mark 5.

Brush a 20cm x 2cm round loose-bottomed tart pan with a little butter. Use a fork to mash the cheeses, thyme, crème fraîche and egg together. Season with salt and pepper.

Place a filo square in the base of the tart pan, letting the excess hang over the sides, and brush with butter. Repeat until all the pastry is used. Place the filling in the centre, spreading out well. Scrunch up the excess pastry and brush the scrunched pastry with the remaining butter. Place on a baking tray and bake for 25 minutes, or until golden. Set aside for 5 minutes to rest, then remove from the pan.

Serves 4

salmon **wellington**

4 sheets frozen puff
  pastry, thawed
2 heaped tbsp basil pesto
4 x 100g skinless salmon fillets
4 cherry tomatoes, thinly sliced
80ml lemon juice, plus extra
  wedges to serve
1 egg, beaten
1 heaped tbsp sesame seeds

Preheat the oven to 200°C/400°F/gas mark 6. Line a baking tray with baking paper.

Halve each sheet of pastry. Spread 2 teaspoons of pesto in the centre of 4 sheets, leaving a 3–4cm pastry border. Place a fish fillet on each and season with salt and pepper. Lay overlapping slices of tomato on top of each salmon fillet. Drizzle with lemon juice and brush the pastry border with some beaten egg.

Cut 4–5 long slits in the centre of the remaining four pastry pieces. Lay each piece of pastry over a salmon fillet, pulling slightly to separate the strips, then press down the edges and trim, making each parcel into a neat rectangle. Brush the pastries with beaten egg and sprinkle with sesame seeds.

Using a fish slice, carefully lift the parcels onto the prepared baking tray, bake for 20–25 minutes, until the fish is just cooked through and the pastry is puffed and golden.

Serves 4

fig & three-cheese tart

6 figs
2 heaped tbsp brown sugar
20ml balsamic vinegar
1 sheet frozen butter puff pastry,
  thawed, halved
100g soft goat's cheese, crumbled
100g grated mozzarella
100g grated Cheddar
4 slices prosciutto
rocket leaves, to serve

Preheat the oven to 180°C/350°F/gas mark 4. Line a baking tray with baking paper.

Place the figs in a small baking dish. Sprinkle with the brown sugar, balsamic vinegar and 2 tablespoons of water. Roast in the oven for 15 minutes. Remove from the oven and set aside to cool.

While the figs are cooling, place the pastry sheets on the prepared baking tray. Lay another piece of baking paper on top. Cover with a second baking tray to weigh the pastry down. Bake in the oven for 15 minutes, or until light golden. Set aside to cool slightly.

Place the goat's cheese, mozzarella and Cheddar in a bowl. Season well. Sprinkle the cheese mixture over the pastry sheets, leaving a 1cm border. Return to the oven for 10 minutes more, or until the cheese is melted and golden. Tear the prosciutto slices into bite-sized pieces and tear the cooled figs in half, reserving the pan juices. Top each tart with half the prosciutto and figs, then top with some rocket leaves. Drizzle with the pan juices from the figs and serve.

Serves 2

5 nights a week
pizza

prosciutto, rocket & tomato pizza

150g buffalo mozzarella*,
    or 4 bocconcini balls
extra virgin olive oil, to drizzle
25g grated Parmesan cheese
8 slices prosciutto, torn
10 cherry tomatoes, halved
50g wild rocket leaves

pizza dough
350g strong (baker's) flour*,
    plus extra to dust
1 tsp caster sugar
7g packet dried instant yeast
40ml olive oil

For the pizza dough, place 250ml warm water in a jug. Place 1 heaped tablespoon of the flour in a bowl with the caster sugar and yeast. Add 60ml of the warm water and stir briefly to combine, then stand in a warm place for 10 minutes, or until large bubbles appear on the surface.

Meanwhile, sift the remaining flour into a large bowl. Add the yeast mixture, olive oil, remaining warm water and 2 teaspoons salt. Bring the mixture together with your hands, then turn onto a lightly floured surface. Knead for 5 minutes, or until the dough is smooth (you can do this stage in an electric mixer with a dough hook). Place the dough in a large, lightly oiled bowl, cover with a damp tea towel and set aside in a warm place to prove for about 1 hour, or until the dough has doubled in size.

Preheat the oven to 200°C/400°F/gas mark 6.

Lightly grease two 26cm pizza trays and dust with a little flour. Turn the dough out onto a floured surface. Knock the air out of the dough with your fist, then divide into two pieces and knead each one into a smooth ball. Dust a rolling pin with flour and roll out the dough into rounds 25cm in diameter. Lay on the prepared pizza trays, then use your hands to press the dough out to the edges of the trays.

Slice the buffalo mozzarella or bocconcini, then lay on paper towel and pat dry to absorb any excess moisture. Drizzle the pizza bases with a little olive oil, then arrange mozzarella and Parmesan on top, followed by the torn prosciutto and cherry-tomato halves. Place the pizzas in the oven and bake for 7 minutes, or until the bases are crisp and golden and the cheese has melted. Remove from the oven and top the pizzas with rocket leaves. Sprinkle with freshly ground black pepper and drizzle with a little more olive oil, then slice and serve immediately.

* Buffalo mozzarella is available from selected delis and gourmet food shops. Strong (baker's) flour is from selected supermarkets and gourmet food shops.

Makes 2 pizzas

pizza with **melted cheese** & **lemon** salad

4 individual plain pizza bases
300g grated mozzarella cheese
40ml lemon juice
80ml olive oil
1 garlic clove, crushed
100g mixed salad leaves with herbs
shaved Parmesan, to serve

Preheat the oven to 220°C/425°F/gas mark 7.

Place the bases on a baking tray and sprinkle with the cheese. Bake for 6 minutes, or until the cheese is melted and golden.

Combine the lemon juice, oil and garlic and season to taste. Toss the mixed salad leaves with the dressing, pile on top of the pizzas just before serving and top with shaved Parmesan.

Serves 4

spicy pepperoni pizza

1 large rectangular pizza base
130g tomato passata (sugo)
1 tsp dried oregano
1 small red onion, thinly sliced
2 buffalo mozzarella balls*
  (or 6 bocconcini), sliced
120g sliced pepperoni
2 heaped tbsp sliced jalapeño
  peppers
olive oil, to drizzle
light sour cream and chopped
  coriander leaves, to serve

Preheat the oven to 190°C/375°F/gas mark 5. Place the pizza base on a large, lightly greased baking sheet.

Spread the pizza base with passata and sprinkle with oregano. Top with onion and mozzarella or bocconcini, followed by pepperoni and jalapeños. Drizzle with olive oil and bake for 15 minutes, or until topping is golden and bubbling. Serve dolloped with sour cream and sprinkled with coriander.

* Buffalo mozzarella is available from selected delis and gourmet food shops.

Serves 4

egg & bacon pizzas

8 thin bacon rashers, rind removed
4 individual pizza bases
5 heaped tbsp sun-dried
   tomato pesto
125g grated mozzarella
4 small eggs
12 cherry tomatoes
olive oil and balsamic vinegar
   (optional), to drizzle
baby rocket leaves, to serve

Preheat the oven to 200°C/400°F/gas mark 6. Line a baking sheet with baking paper, then spread the bacon out in a single layer. Cook in the oven for 5–6 minutes, until just starting to crisp.

Remove the baking paper and lightly oil the baking sheet. Place the pizza bases on the sheet and spread with the sun-dried tomato pesto. Lay 2 bacon rashers on each pizza and sprinkle cheese over the bacon. Carefully break an egg into the centre of each pizza, then sit 3 cherry tomatoes to one side of the egg. Drizzle each pizza with olive oil, season with salt and pepper, then bake for 6 minutes, or until the egg has just cooked and the tomatoes have started to wilt. Scatter with rocket and drizzle with a little balsamic vinegar.

Serves 4

maple-glazed **squash** & **blue cheese** pizzas

unsalted butter, for greasing
500g butterball squash
   or pumpkin
1 tsp chilli flakes
1 tsp cumin seeds
60ml olive oil
60ml pure maple syrup
2 pizza bases
100g grated mozzarella
100g mild blue cheese, crumbled
100g rocket leaves
20ml balsamic vinegar

Preheat the oven to 200°C/400°F/gas mark 6. Lightly grease a baking tray with butter.

Cut the squash into 1.5cm-thick slices. Spread on the baking tray, rub with the chilli, cumin, oil and syrup, then season. Roast for 20 minutes, then turn and roast for a further 10 minutes.

Meanwhile, place the pizza bases on a large baking tray and scatter with mozzarella. Place in the oven for the final 6-8 minutes of the squash cooking time, until the cheese is bubbling and the bases are crisp. Place the squash slices on the bases (reserving the pan juices), scatter with blue cheese and return to the oven for 2–3 minutes. Remove from the oven and scatter with rocket.

Stir the balsamic vinegar into the squash roasting juices and drizzle over the pizzas before serving.

Serves 4

5 nights a week
sausages

maple bangers & mustard mash

150ml maple syrup
4 heaped tbsp honey
   wholegrain mustard
1 onion, halved, thinly sliced
16 (about 500g) beef
   chipolata sausages
4 potatoes (such as desiree),
   peeled, halved
30g unsalted butter
80ml thin cream
2 heaped tbsp chopped
   flat-leaf parsley

Preheat the oven to 180°C/350°F/gas mark 4.

In a small bowl, combine the maple syrup with half of the honey mustard and 80ml water.

Sprinkle the onion over the base of a baking tray. Place the sausages on top and pour over the maple-syrup mixture. Roast for 30 minutes, basting with the pan juices from time to time and turning the sausages halfway through cooking.

Meanwhile, cook the potatoes in a large saucepan of boiling salted water until tender, then drain well. Return to the pan with the butter and cream, and mash well. Season to taste with salt and freshly ground black pepper. Stir in the parsley and the remaining mustard.

Serve the sausages on the mustard mash, topped with the onions and drizzled with the pan juices.

Serves 4

sausage, **pea** & **feta** salad

250g new potatoes
8 good-quality chicken or lamb sausages
400g frozen peas
1 red onion, sliced
60g mint leaves
2 heaped tbsp chopped flat-leaf parsley
80ml olive oil
40ml lemon juice
200g marinated feta, drained

Cook the potatoes in boiling salted water until tender, then drain. Meanwhile, preheat a grill or barbecue to a medium heat and cook the sausages for 5–6 minutes, until golden and cooked. Thickly slice the sausages and halve the potatoes.

Cook the peas in boiling salted water for 3 minutes, then drain and refresh in cold water. Place in a large bowl or platter with the sausages, potato and remaining ingredients. Season, toss and serve.

Serves 4

spicy stuffed sausage & cheese croissants

20ml olive oil
1 onion, finely chopped
350g spicy sausages (such as chorizo),
   meat removed from casings
200g button mushrooms, chopped
1 heaped tbsp tomato paste
100ml red wine
410g canned chopped tomatoes
75g semi-dried tomatoes
4 large croissants
80g grated Cheddar

Preheat the oven to 180°C/350°F/gas mark 4.

Heat the oil in a frying pan over a medium heat, add the onion and cook for 2–3 minutes to soften. Add the sausage meat and mushrooms and cook for 5 minutes, breaking up the meat. Add the tomato paste and wine and cook for 2–3 minutes, until most of the wine has evaporated. Add all the tomatoes and cook, stirring, for 5–6 minutes, until very little of the liquid remains.

Cut deep slashes in the top of the croissants. Fill with the mixture. Place on a baking tray, top with cheese and bake for 5–6 minutes, until the croissants are hot and the cheese has melted.

Serves 4

rigatoni **milano**

40ml olive oil
2 red onions, sliced
500g good-quality Italian sausages,
    meat removed from casings
2 garlic cloves, crushed
1 heaped tbsp chopped fresh
    rosemary leaves
¼ tsp dried chilli flakes
250ml tomato passata (sugo)
250ml beef stock
400g rigatoni pasta
5 tbsp chopped flat-leaf parsley leaves
100ml double cream
80g grated Parmesan, to serve

Heat the oil in a large pan over a medium heat. Add the onion and cook, stirring occasionally, for 5 minutes, or until light golden. Add the sausage meat and garlic to the pan and cook for 3–4 minutes, breaking the meat up with a wooden spoon, until browned. Add the rosemary, chilli, passata and stock. Season, reduce the heat to low and cook for 15–20 minutes, until the meat is cooked.

Meanwhile, cook the pasta according to the packet instructions. Drain and add to the sauce. Stir the parsley and cream into the sauce just before serving. Scatter with Parmesan.

Serves 4

barbecued frankfurters with coleslaw

2 tsp horseradish
90g sour cream
20ml lemon juice
1 heaped tbsp Dijon mustard
300g red cabbage, shredded
2 carrots, grated
2 heaped tbsp chopped dill
8 Vienna frankfurters
olive oil, to brush
tomato sauce and buttered
  wholemeal rolls, to serve

Soak 16 skewers in cold water for 20 minutes to prevent them from burning. (Omit the skewers if you don't have time.)

For the coleslaw, whisk the horseradish, sour cream, lemon juice and mustard in a large bowl and season. Add the cabbage, carrot and dill, then toss and set aside.

Heat a griddle pan or barbecue to high. Halve the frankfurters, thread onto the skewers if using, and brush with oil. Cook, turning, for 2–3 minutes, until heated through and beginning to brown. Serve with the coleslaw, tomato sauce and buttered wholemeal rolls.

Serves 4

5 nights a week
mince

rice noodles with sweet-chilli meatballs

oil, for greasing
800g pork mince
2–3cm piece ginger, grated
2 garlic cloves, finely chopped
60ml sweet chilli sauce,
    plus extra to serve
4 tbsp finely chopped coriander
    leaves
200g thin rice stick noodles
    (vermicelli)
½ cucumber, thickly sliced
1 small red onion, sliced
5 tbsp mint leaves

Preheat the oven to 180°C/350°F/gas mark 4.

Lightly grease a baking tray. Use your hands to mix the pork, ginger, garlic, 20ml sweet chilli sauce and half the coriander in a bowl. Roll into walnut-sized balls then bake on the tray for 20 minutes, or until golden.

Place the remaining sauce in a bowl. Use tongs to dip the meatballs in the sauce to coat, then return them to the oven for 5 minutes.

Meanwhile, cook the noodles according to the packet instructions. Drain and refresh in cold water. Combine the cucumber, onion and mint. Divide the noodles among serving bowls. Serve topped with the meatballs and cucumber mix, with extra sauce to drizzle if desired.

Serves 3–4

chilli beef on avocado

20ml olive oil
1 large onion, finely chopped
500g beef mince
400g can chopped tomatoes
125ml beef stock or water
2 heaped tbsp tomato paste
1 heaped tbsp cocoa powder
1 tsp chilli powder
1 tsp dried oregano
420g can red kidney beans,
    rinsed, drained
2 avocados
steamed white rice, thinly sliced red
    onion, coriander sprigs and corn
    chips, to serve

Heat the olive oil in a large frying pan over a medium-high heat. Add the onion and cook for 2–3 minutes, until soft. Increase the heat to high, then add the beef mince and cook, stirring, for 4–5 minutes, until browned. Reduce the heat to medium, then stir in the tomatoes, beef stock, tomato paste, cocoa powder, chilli powder and oregano, and simmer for 15 minutes. Add the kidney beans and cook for 5 minutes, or until they are heated through.

Meanwhile, halve the avocados and remove the stones and peel. Divide the rice among serving bowls and top with the avocado halves. Top with the chilli beef, and garnish with the onion and coriander. Serve with corn chips.

Serves 4

satay beef lettuce parcels

20ml peanut oil
1 large onion, finely chopped
500g lean beef mince
4 heaped tbsp peanut satay sauce
80ml beef stock
20ml dark soy sauce
35g coriander leaves, plus extra
   to garnish
12 large lettuce leaves
½ cucumber, peeled, chopped
40g roasted peanuts, chopped

Heat the oil in a wok or frying pan over a medium heat. Add the onion and beef and cook for 5–6 minutes, until the meat is browned all over. Stir in the satay sauce, stock and soy sauce. Cook for a further minute, then add the coriander.

Serve the beef in the lettuce leaves garnished with cucumber, peanuts and extra coriander.

Serves 4

home-style **doner kebab**

oil, for greasing
500g lean lamb mince
3 garlic cloves, crushed
1 heaped tbsp plain flour
40ml olive oil
2 heaped tbsp chopped flat-leaf parsley
2 tsp ground cumin
2 tsp ground cinnamon
3 tsp ground coriander
1 egg, beaten
lemon, warmed pitta bread, salad,
    natural yoghurt and mint, to serve

Preheat the grill to a medium-high heat. Line the base of a 28cm x 8cm baking tray with baking paper and lightly grease.

Combine the lamb, garlic, flour, oil, parsley, spices, egg, and salt and pepper to taste in a bowl. Press into an even layer in the pan.

Place the pan under the grill for 4 minutes, or until lightly browned. Drain off any liquid, then invert onto a board. Discard the paper, then return the meat to the pan, sealed-side down, and grill for 2 minutes, until cooked through. Slice the meat into thin strips, squeeze over the lemon, then pack into pitta bread with salad, yoghurt and mint.

Serves 4

quick pasta & meatballs

500g good-quality pork and
  herb sausages, meat removed
  from casings
520g tomato passata (sugo)
250ml chicken stock
400g rigatoni or penne pasta
20ml olive oil
sliced basil leaves and grated
  Parmesan, to serve

Preheat the oven to 180°C/350°F/gas mark 4. Line a baking tray with baking paper.

Roll the sausage meat into small balls about 2cm across. Spread the meatballs in a single layer on the baking tray and cook in the oven for 15 minutes, or until golden.

While the meatballs are baking, place the tomato passata and chicken stock in a large saucepan over a medium heat. Season well with sea salt and freshly ground black pepper, then simmer over a medium heat for 5 minutes, or until slightly reduced. Remove the meatballs from the oven and drain off any excess fat. Add the meatballs to the sauce and leave to simmer over a medium-low heat for 10 minutes, or until the sauce thickens.

Meanwhile, cook the pasta in a large saucepan of boiling salted water according to the packet instructions, then drain and toss with the olive oil.

Divide the pasta among plates, top with some meatballs and sauce, and serve with basil and Parmesan.

Serves 4

5 nights a week
burgers

tuscan burgers

600g beef mince
100g pancetta, rind removed, chopped
5 tbsp basil pesto
2 small red onions, thickly sliced
40ml olive oil
2 small vine-ripened tomatoes,
   thickly sliced
150g whole-egg mayonnaise
3–4 bocconcini, sliced
4 Italian-style bread rolls, split
50g baby rocket leaves

Place the beef, pancetta and half of the pesto in a processor. Season with salt and pepper. Pulse until just combined (do not over process). Form the mixture into four patties and chill while you cook the vegetables.

Preheat the oven to 170°C/325°F/gas mark 3.

Heat a griddle pan or barbecue to a medium heat. Toss the onion in a little oil and grill for 1 minute each side, or until just cooked. Place in the oven to keep warm.

Brush the tomatoes with a little oil and season, then grill for 1 minute each side. Place in the oven to keep warm.

Brush both sides of the patties with oil. Cook on the griddle for 2–3 minutes each side, until cooked through.

Mix the remaining pesto with the mayonnaise.

Top the patties with cheese and place in the oven for 1 minute, or until the cheese melts.

Spread the bread-roll bases with some of the mayonnaise mixture. Top with the rocket, patties, onion and tomato. Drizzle with the remaining mayonnaise mixture and top with the remaining bread-roll halves.

Serves 4

mushroom & goat's cheese panini

60ml extra virgin olive oil,
    plus extra to drizzle
2 red onions, finely sliced
20ml balsamic vinegar
4 large field mushrooms,
    stalks removed
75g chopped sun-dried tomatoes
    in olive oil
100g soft goat's cheese, cut into
    4 slices (or crumbled)
4 thin slices prosciutto, cut into
    4cm-long pieces
4 round rustic rolls
50g wild rocket leaves, to serve

Preheat the oven to 180°C/350°F/gas mark 4. Lightly grease a baking tray.

Heat 40ml of the oil in a frying pan, add the onion and cook over a low heat for 10 minutes, stirring occasionally, until softened and beginning to caramelise. Add the balsamic vinegar and cook for a further 5 minutes, stirring occasionally.

Place the mushrooms upside down on the baking tray, drizzle with the remaining olive oil and place in the oven for 10 minutes, until almost cooked through.

Stir the sun-dried tomatoes into the onion mixture along with salt and freshly ground black pepper. Spoon the mixture into the mushroom cups, cover with slices of goat's cheese and top with the prosciutto. Return to the oven and bake for a further 10 minutes, until the cheese is tinged golden. Split the rolls in half and arrange some rocket leaves on the base of each one. Place a mushroom on top and drizzle with a little extra virgin olive oil.

Serves 4

lamb burgers with beetroot salsa

500g lamb mince
1 red onion, finely chopped
1 garlic clove, chopped
3 tbsp flat-leaf parsley leaves
3 tsp ground cumin
160g mint leaves, plus extra
   to garnish
425g canned baby
   beetroot, drained
1 tbsp finely chopped
   coriander leaves
60ml lemon juice
60ml olive oil, plus extra
   for frying
100g soft goat's cheese
toasted hamburger buns and
   salad leaves, to serve

Place the lamb in the bowl of a food processor with half the onion, the garlic, parsley, 2 teaspoons of the cumin and half of the mint. Pulse until the mixture just comes together. Season with salt and pepper and form into four patties.

Cut the beetroot into small cubes. Place in a bowl with the remaining onion, cumin and mint. Add the coriander, lemon juice and oil, then season and set aside.

Preheat the grill to high.

Lightly oil a frying pan or griddle and heat over a medium-high heat. Cook the patties to your liking. Crumble the cheese on top of each patty. Place under the grill for about 1 minute, until the cheese is bubbling.

Serve the burgers on toasted buns with salad leaves, beetroot salsa and extra mint leaves.

Serves 4

curried vegetable burgers

40ml olive oil
1 onion, finely chopped
1 garlic clove, crushed
2 courgettes, grated
1 large carrot, grated
100g (about 4 slices) wholemeal bread,
    crusts removed
400g canned chickpeas, rinsed, drained
3 tsp mild curry paste
4 tbsp crunchy peanut butter
1 egg yolk
4 tbsp chopped coriander leaves,
    plus extra leaves to serve
6 bread rolls (we used sesame seed)
mayonnaise, chutney, lettuce and tomato,
    to serve

Heat half the oil in a large frying pan over a medium-low heat, add the onion and cook for 5 minutes, or until softened. Add the garlic, courgette and carrot and cook, stirring, for 2–3 minutes, until wilted and softened. Drain off any liquid.

Place the bread and chickpeas in the bowl of a food processor and pulse to combine. Add the softened vegetables, curry paste, peanut butter, yolk and coriander. Process until the mixture comes together.

Form the mixture into six patties and chill for 10 minutes. Heat the remaining oil in a non-stick frying pan over a medium heat and cook the burgers, in batches if necessary, for 1–2 minutes each side, until golden. Serve in rolls with mayonnaise, chutney, lettuce, tomato and extra coriander leaves.

Serves 6

lamb burgers with feta & tomato

40ml olive oil, plus extra for frying
20ml lemon juice
160g mint leaves
500g lamb mince
5 tbsp ready-made olive tapenade
200g feta, cut into 8 thin slices
2 vine-ripened tomatoes, sliced
100g rocket
½ cucumber, cut into wedges
4 rounds pitta bread, warmed
thick yoghurt, to serve

To make the dressing, mix together the oil and lemon juice, season and set aside.

For the burgers, chop half the mint and mix in a bowl with the lamb and tapenade. Don't season, as the tapenade will be salty. Form eight small burgers.

Heat the extra oil in a frying pan over a medium-high heat. Add the burgers and cook for 2–3 minutes on each side (in batches if necessary). Remove, then top each burger with a slice of feta, a slice of tomato and a mint leaf. Repeat with the another burger and another feta and tomato slice. Secure with a toothpick if necessary.

In a bowl, toss the rocket, cucumber and the remaining mint together with half the dressing. Place some warm pitta bread on each plate, sit a burger stack on top and some salad on the side.

Drizzle with the remaining dressing and serve with a dollop of yoghurt. Season with black pepper.

Serves 4

5 nights a week
fish

swordfish with italian parsley salad & garlic mash

4 x 200g swordfish steaks
100ml olive oil, plus extra to brush
160g roughly chopped flat-leaf
    parsley leaves
2 heaped tbsp capers, rinsed,
    drained, chopped
75g sliced pitted green olives
zest and juice of 1 lemon

garlic mash
1kg floury potatoes (such as
    King Edward), peeled, chopped
4 garlic cloves
80ml milk
60ml olive oil

For the mash, place the potatoes and garlic in a pan of cold salted water. Bring to the boil, then cook over a medium heat until tender. Drain well, then return to the pan and shake over a low heat to remove excess water. Mash the potato and garlic with the milk and oil, then season well. Keep warm until ready to serve.

Brush the fish with the extra oil, season well and pat with a little of the parsley.

Place the capers, olives, zest and juice in a bowl with the remaining parsley. Season with pepper and slowly whisk in the oil.

Preheat a griddle pan or barbecue to a high heat and cook the fish for 2 minutes each side, until seared but still pink in the middle, or until cooked to your liking.

Serve the fish with the garlic mash and topped with the parsley salad.

Serves 4

sweet-&-sour fish with **pineapple** rice

20ml sunflower oil
1 red pepper, thinly sliced
1 yellow pepper, thinly sliced
2cm piece of ginger, peeled,
  cut into matchsticks
1 long red chilli, seeds removed,
  finely chopped
150g cherry tomatoes, halved
60ml honey
60ml white wine vinegar
4 x 200g skinless firm white fish fillets
  (such as John Dory or haddock),
  pin-boned (ask your fishmonger
  to do this for you)
4 spring onions, thinly sliced on the
  diagonal, to garnish

pineapple rice
150g basmati and wild rice blend*
165g fresh pineapple, chopped
1 long red chilli, seeds
  removed, chopped
40ml fish sauce
1 heaped tbsp chopped coriander

For the pineapple rice, cook the rice in a pan of boiling salted water according to the packet instructions, until tender. Drain, then cover and keep warm.

Heat the oil in a frying pan over a medium-high heat. Add the red and yellow peppers and cook for 2–3 minutes, until starting to soften. Add the ginger, chilli and tomatoes, and stir for 1–2 minutes. Stir in the honey and vinegar.

Meanwhile, line a steamer with baking paper. Place the fish fillets, in a single layer, in the steamer. Cover and steam over a saucepan of simmering water for 6–8 minutes, until just cooked.

Just before serving, toss with the pineapple, chilli, fish sauce and coriander. Divide the rice among serving plates. Top with the steamed fish, then spoon over the sauce and garnish with spring onion.

* Available from selected supermarkets and gourmet food shops.

Serves 4

steamed fish with black-bean sauce

4 x 150g firm white fish fillets
   (such as John Dory or snapper),
   skin on
2.5cm piece ginger, cut into thin strips
8 spring onions, cut finely into
   10cm lengths
sesame oil, to drizzle
170g can black beans*, drained
40ml black-bean sauce
40ml Chinese rice wine*
20ml soy sauce
2 heaped tbsp caster sugar
350g mange-tout

Line a bamboo steamer with a sheet of baking paper and place the fish fillets on the base of steamer. Combine the ginger and spring onions. Use half the mixture to spread over the fillets; reserve the remaining ginger and spring onions. Season the fish, then drizzle with a little sesame oil.

Place the black beans, black-bean sauce, rice wine, soy sauce and sugar in a pan and bring to the boil. Reduce the heat to low and simmer for 1–2 minutes.

Meanwhile, place the steamer over a pan of simmering water and cook the fish for 5 minutes. Add the mange-tout and reserved ginger and spring onions and steam for a further minute. Place a pile of mange-tout, ginger and spring onions on each plate, top with the fish and drizzle with the black-bean sauce.

* Black beans and Chinese rice wine (shaohsing) are available from Asian supermarkets. Substitute Chinese rice wine with dry sherry.

Serves 4

harissa fish with fattoush

4 tbsp harissa*
80ml lemon juice, plus wedges
  to serve
4 x 180g skinless firm white fish
  fillets (such as John Dory)
1 cucumber, peeled, seeds
  removed, cut into chunks
3 tomatoes, seeds removed,
  cut into chunks
120g watercress sprigs
1 small red onion, sliced
160g kalamata olives
100ml olive oil
2 tsp sumac*
1 pitta bread, grilled until crisp

**Fattoush is a traditional Middle Eastern salad with crisp
pitta bread.**

Combine the harissa and half the lemon juice in a ceramic
dish. Add the fish, turn to coat, then set aside while you make
the fattoush.

Place the cucumber, tomato, watercress, onion and olives in a
bowl. Mix 80ml of the oil, the sumac and the remaining lemon
juice in another small bowl. Season and set aside while you
cook the fish.

Heat the remaining oil in a large non-stick frying pan over a
medium heat. Cook the fish for 3–4 minutes each side, or
until golden and cooked through.

Break the pitta bread into pieces and toss with the salad and
dressing. Serve the fish on the salad, with lemon wedges.

* Harissa and sumac (which has a citrus flavour) are available from selected
supermarkets and Middle Eastern shops.

Serves 4

trout with dill potatoes & beetroot pesto

225g can beetroot, drained
grated zest of 1 orange
50g Parmesan, grated
2 garlic cloves
1 heaped tbsp horseradish cream
4 tbsp dill fronds
80ml olive oil
120ml light sour cream
2 tsp wholegrain mustard
600g cooked small potatoes
4 x 180g trout fillets, skin on

Chop the beetroot, orange zest, Parmesan, garlic, half the horseradish and half the dill in a food processor. Slowly add 60ml oil until you have a coarse purée. Set aside.

In a bowl, whisk the sour cream, mustard, the remaining horseradish and remaining dill. Season with salt and pepper. Slice the potatoes and toss them in the sour-cream dressing.

Heat the remaining oil in a large non-stick frying pan over a medium-high heat. Fry the fish, skin-side down, for 3–4 minutes, until crisp, then turn over, reduce the heat to medium and cook for 2–3 minutes, until just cooked through. Divide the potatoes among plates, top with the fish and a dollop of beetroot pesto, then serve.

Serves 4

5 nights a week
seafood

thai-style **bouillabaisse**

2 tsp vegetable oil
3 tbsp Thai green curry paste
2 x 400ml cans coconut milk
zest and juice of 1 lime,
  plus extra wedges, to serve
3 kaffir lime leaves*
40ml fish sauce
500g good-quality seafood
  marinara mix
2 heaped tbsp coriander leaves
steamed jasmine rice, to serve

Heat the oil in a large deep frying pan over a medium heat. Cook the green curry paste, stirring, for 1 minute, until fragrant. Add the coconut milk, lime zest and juice, kaffir lime leaves and fish sauce. Simmer for 5 minutes, then add the seafood marinara mix and simmer for a further 5 minutes, or until the seafood is cooked, discarding any shellfish that remain unopened.

Stir in the coriander leaves, then serve the bouillabaisse with steamed rice and lime wedges to squeeze.

* Kaffir lime leaves are available from selected greengrocers and Asian food shops.

Serves 4

seafood stew with rouille

20ml olive oil
1 onion, thinly sliced
2 garlic cloves, crushed
400g waxy potatoes (such as
  kipfler), peeled, sliced
½ tsp saffron
250ml white wine
2 heaped tbsp sun-dried
  tomato paste
400g can crushed tomatoes
300ml fish stock
1 heaped tbsp chopped fresh
  rosemary
300g firm white fish fillet (such as
  haddock), cut into pieces
400g black mussels, scrubbed,
  debearded
toasted baguette and chopped
  flat-leaf parsley, to serve

rouille*
1 roasted red pepper*
1 potato, peeled, boiled, chopped
2 garlic cloves, chopped
1 egg yolk
125ml olive oil

Heat the oil in a large pan over a medium heat. Add the onion and cook for 1 minute, until softened. Add the crushed garlic, potato, saffron and wine and simmer for 2 minutes. Add the tomato paste, tomatoes, stock and rosemary and cook for 15 minutes.

To make the rouille, place the roasted pepper, potato, garlic and egg yolk in a food processor and season with salt and pepper. Process to combine, then add the oil in a thin steady stream until you have a smooth emulsion.

Season the stew with salt and pepper, then add the fish and mussels. Cover and cook for a further 5 minutes. Remove the lid and discard any unopened mussels. Serve the stew with the toasted baguette and a dollop of rouille on top, scattered with parsley.

* Rouille is a red, mayonnaise-like sauce which is a speciality of Provence, France. Keep covered in the fridge for 3–4 days. Roasted pepper is available from delis and selected supermarkets.

Serves 4

sushi **rice** & **prawn** salad

400g Japanese sushi rice,
  rinsed, drained
1kg cooked tiger prawns,
  peeled, deveined
2 cucumbers, peeled, halved
  lengthways, thinly sliced
2 small red chillies, seeds removed,
  thinly sliced into strips
4 spring onions, thinly sliced on
  the diagonal
2 tsp black or regular sesame seeds

dressing
40ml mirin*
60ml rice vinegar
20ml soy sauce
2 tsp sesame oil
juice of 1 lemon

Place the rice and 500ml water in a saucepan and bring to the boil. Season with salt and cover with a tight-fitting lid. Reduce the heat to very low and cook for 10 minutes, or until the water has been absorbed. Remove from the heat and stand for 5 minutes.

Meanwhile, whisk the dressing ingredients in a large bowl and add the remaining salad ingredients. Fluff the rice with a fork, then toss with the salad. Serve warm.

* Mirin is available from selected supermarkets and Asian food shops.

Serves 4

250g rice vermicelli
20ml peanut oil
5 tbsp good-quality laksa paste*
750ml fish or vegetable stock
400ml coconut milk
750g prawns, deveined, shelled,
   tails on
250g scallops
100g deep-fried tofu*, quartered
100g bean sprouts, trimmed
20g each fresh coriander, Vietnamese
   mint* and Thai basil* leaves,
   plus extra to serve
1 small red chilli, seeds removed,
   cut into thin strips
2 heaped tbsp chopped peanuts,
   to serve
fried Asian shallots*, to garnish

Place the vermicelli in a bowl, cover with boiling water and leave for 10 minutes to soak. Drain and set aside.

Heat the oil in a wok over a medium-high heat. Add the laksa paste and stir-fry for 1 minute. Stir in the stock, bring to the boil, then add the coconut milk and simmer for 2 minutes. Add the prawns, scallops and deep-fried tofu and cook for 2 minutes. Season with 1 teaspoon salt.

Divide the noodles among serving bowls, top with the bean sprouts and the fresh herbs. Pour the laksa soup over the noodles, dividing the seafood equally among the bowls. Garnish with slices of chilli, the peanuts, shallots and the extra herbs.

* Available from Asian supermarkets. If the Vietnamese mint and Thai basil are unavailable, substitute with extra fresh coriander.

Serves 4

tikka prawns with yoghurt pilaf

3 tbsp tikka or mild curry paste
6 tbsp thick Greek yoghurt
4 heaped tbsp chopped coriander,
    plus extra leaves to garnish
12 large king prawns
6 cardamom pods, lightly crushed
200g basmati rice

Combine 2 tablespoons curry paste, 5 tablespoons yoghurt and 3 tablespoons coriander in a large shallow dish. Add the prawns and turn to coat. Cover and refrigerate until needed.

Place the remaining tablespoon of curry paste, the cardamom and 1 teaspoon salt in a large pan. Add the rice and 375ml cold water, stirring to distribute the paste. Bring to the boil, then reduce the heat to low and simmer, partially covered, for 10 minutes, or until most of the liquid has been absorbed. Stir in the remaining tablespoon of yoghurt and coriander, and cover to keep warm.

Preheat a griddle pan or barbecue to a high heat. Cook the prawns for 1–2 minutes each side, until cooked through.

Sprinkle the pilaf with extra coriander and serve the prawns with the pilaf.

Serves 4

5 nights a week
chicken

easy chicken & artichoke rice

25g unsalted butter
20ml olive oil
2 leeks (white part only),
   finely chopped
1 bay leaf
1 garlic clove, crushed
pared rind and juice of 1 lemon,
   plus extra wedges, to serve
2 x 180g skinless chicken breast fillets,
   cut into thin strips
250g basmati rice
500ml chicken or vegetable stock
2 heaped tbsp chopped basil leaves
6–8 chargrilled artichoke
   hearts, quartered

Melt the butter with the oil in a large saucepan over a low heat. Add the leeks, bay leaf and garlic and cook for about 5 minutes, stirring occasionally, or until the leeks soften.

Add the lemon rind and the chicken to the saucepan and cook, stirring, for about 5 minutes, or until the chicken is opaque. Add the rice, stirring well to coat the grains, then add the stock and half the lemon juice. Increase the heat and bring to the boil, then reduce the heat to low, cover and cook for 12 minutes. Remove from the heat and leave covered for a further 10 minutes.

Stir in the chopped basil, artichoke hearts and the remaining lemon juice. Serve with freshly ground black pepper and some lemon wedges.

Serves 4–6

chicken tonnato

4 (about 140g each) skinless
  corn-fed chicken breast fillets
  (wingbone attached, optional)
125ml light olive oil,
  plus extra to brush
80g pitted kalamata olives
20ml lemon juice
250ml mayonnaise
95g can tuna in spring
  water, drained
2 heaped tbsp salted capers,
  rinsed
100g wild rocket leaves,
  rinsed, dried

Preheat the oven to 200ºC/400ºF/gas mark 6.

Lay baking paper on the base of a roasting tray and place the chicken breasts on top. Brush with a little olive oil, season and roast for 10 minutes, or until just cooked. Remove from the oven and cover with a piece of foil. Set aside to rest.

Place 125ml olive oil, the olives and lemon juice in a food processor and process to combine (don't over-process; it should retain some texture). Set aside. Clean the processor and place the mayonnaise, drained tuna, 1 teaspoon of capers and 40ml of warm water in the processor. Process until smooth.

To serve, divide the tuna sauce among plates, slice the chicken breasts on the diagonal and place on top. Toss the rocket in half the olive dressing and place on top of the chicken, sprinkle with the remaining capers and drizzle with the remaining olive dressing. Serve at room temperature.

Serves 4

chicken & **pepper tortillas**

2 (about 120g each) skinless
  chicken breast fillets
1 small red pepper
1 small yellow pepper
1 Spanish onion
grated zest and juice of 1 lime
1 small red chilli, finely chopped
40ml vegetable oil
8 flour tortillas
60g chopped coriander leaves
260g hummus
lettuce leaves and sour cream,
  to serve

Cut the chicken, red and yellow peppers and onion into thin strips and place in a bowl. Add the lime zest, chilli and oil and season with salt and pepper. Toss to combine.

Warm the tortillas following the packet directions.

Heat a griddle pan to high. When it is hot, add the chicken mixture and cook for 2–3 minutes, until charred (you may need to do this in batches; if so, keep the cooked batch warm in the oven). Stir in the lime juice and half the coriander.

Spread the tortillas with hummus, top with lettuce leaves, the chicken and scatter with the remaining coriander. Serve with the sour cream.

Serves 4

chicken **pizzaiola**

40ml olive oil
4 chicken breast fillets (with skin
  and wing-bone attached, optional)
1 small onion, thinly sliced
2 garlic cloves, crushed
1 red pepper, thinly sliced
1 yellow pepper, thinly sliced
125g small button mushrooms, sliced
4 Roma tomatoes, blanched, peeled,
  seeds removed, chopped
1 tsp tomato paste
1 heaped tbsp chopped fresh oregano,
  plus extra to garnish
125ml white wine
125ml chicken stock
4 slices provolone piccante cheese*

Preheat the oven to 180°C/350°F/gas mark 4.

Heat 20ml of oil in a large non-stick frying pan on a medium-high heat. Season the chicken and cook for 2 minutes on each side, until golden. Roast on a baking tray for 10 minutes, until cooked.

Meanwhile, heat the remaining oil in the same pan over a medium heat. Cook the onion for 5 minutes, then add the garlic, red and yellow peppers and mushrooms. Cook for 5 minutes more. Add the tomatoes, tomato paste and oregano and cook for 5 minutes. Add the white wine and chicken stock, bring to the boil, then reduce the heat and simmer for 5 minutes to thicken slightly.

Top the chicken with the cheese slices, then melt in the oven for 1 minute. Serve topped with sauce and garnished with extra oregano.

* Available from good Italian delis. Substitute mozzarella.

Serves 4

chicken with avocado & pink grapefruit salad

2 pink grapefruit
1 large avocado, peeled, cut
  into wedges
250g bunch watercress,
  stalks trimmed
6 chicken breast fillets (with skin)
50ml olive oil, plus extra to brush
½ tsp caster sugar
40ml lemon juice
2 heaped tbsp slivered pistachio
  kernels*
250ml thick Greek yoghurt

Preheat the oven to 180°C/350°F/gas mark 4.

Remove the grapefruit peel and pith. Holding the fruit in your hand (over a bowl to catch the juice), cut the segments away from the membrane with a small knife. Squeeze the remains to catch the extra juice, then set the juice aside and place the segments in a bowl with the avocado and watercress.

Brush the chicken with the extra oil and season. Cook in a large frying pan over a high heat for 1–2 minutes each side, until golden. Place on a baking tray and roast for 5–6 minutes, until cooked.

Meanwhile, whisk the oil, sugar and half the lemon juice into the grapefruit juice. Season, then toss with the salad and nuts. Mix the remaining lemon juice with the yoghurt and season. Slice the chicken thickly and serve with the salad and lemon yoghurt.

* Available from delis and gourmet food shops. Substitute pistachio kernels, chopped.

Serves 6

5 nights a week
beef

quick beef **stroganoff**

600g fillet steak, thinly sliced
2 tbsp flour
2 tsp smoked paprika (pimentón)*
30ml olive oil
1 heaped tbsp unsalted butter
1 large onion, finely sliced
2 garlic cloves, crushed
2 tsp chopped thyme
250g button mushrooms, sliced
60ml brandy
150ml beef stock
300ml sour cream
2 heaped tbsp chopped flat-leaf
  parsley, to garnish
boiled waxy potatoes (such as kipfler)
  and pickled gherkins, to serve

Toss the meat in a bowl with the flour and paprika to coat. Heat the oil in a large frying pan over a high heat and fry the steak quickly in batches for 1–2 minutes, or until seared on all sides. Remove and set aside.

Reduce the heat to medium-high, add the butter and sliced onion and cook for a few minutes until the onion starts to soften and colour. Add the garlic and cook for 30 seconds. Add the thyme and mushrooms and cook for 2 minutes. Stir in the brandy and stock and allow to bubble for a further minute. Stir in the sour cream, steak and any meat juices, then season with salt and pepper. Garnish with parsley and serve with the potatoes and gherkins.

* Smoked paprika is available from gourmet food shops and delis.

Serves 4

beef **braciole**

6 x 1cm-thick slices Scotch fillet
    or topside steak, trimmed
2 heaped tbsp finely chopped
    flat-leaf parsley
2 garlic cloves, crushed
2 heaped tbsp finely grated
    Parmesan cheese
2 heaped tbsp toasted pine nuts
6 slices prosciutto, halved widthways
40ml olive oil
125ml dry red wine
520g tomato passata (sugo)
4 tbsp sliced basil leaves, shredded
cooked, soft polenta (optional), to serve

Using a meat tenderiser or a rolling pin, pound the steaks between sheets of baking paper until they are about 5mm thick. Cut the steaks in two widthways. (You can ask your butcher to do this for you.)

Combine the parsley, garlic, Parmesan and pine nuts in a small bowl. Season with sea salt and black pepper.

Lay the prosciutto slices over each steak and scatter with the parsley mixture. Roll up to enclose the mixture and secure with toothpicks.

Heat the oil in a large frying pan over a medium-high heat and cook the rolls for 3–4 minutes, turning, until browned all over. Transfer to a plate and cover loosely with foil to keep warm.

Add the wine to the hot pan and boil until reduced by half. Add the passata and bring to the boil, then simmer over a low heat for 5 minutes, or until thickened. Season to taste with sea salt and freshly ground black pepper. Return the rolls and any juices to the pan, then scatter with basil and cook for 3 minutes, or until heated through. Slice the rolls in half and serve with soft polenta.

Serves 4

steak with lemony **puttanesca** sauce

2 heaped tbsp chopped
   fresh thyme
1 tsp cumin seeds
2 heaped tbsp oregano
   leaves
4 garlic cloves
zest and juice of 1 lemon,
   plus 2 extra lemons,
   to serve
60ml extra virgin olive oil
4 (about 200g each)
   sirloin steaks
½ tsp chilli flakes
4 anchovy fillets
400g can chopped tomatoes
8 pitted kalamata olives,
   quartered
1 heaped tbsp salted capers,
   rinsed
mashed potato, to serve

Place the thyme, cumin seeds, oregano, 2 garlic cloves and
1 teaspoon sea salt in a mortar and crush together well with
a pestle. Add half the lemon zest and 40ml olive oil. Flatten
the steaks slightly with a rolling pin, then rub in the marinade.
Set aside for 20 minutes to marinate.

Heat the remaining oil in a saucepan. Crush the remaining
garlic and add it to the oil with the chilli and anchovies. Cook for
1 minute over a medium heat, mashing the anchovies into the oil.
Add the tomatoes, remaining lemon zest and 40ml of lemon juice.
Cook over a low heat for 5–6 minutes. Add the olives and capers
and simmer for 2 minutes.

Heat a griddle pan over a high heat. When it's hot, add the steaks
and cook for 2–3 minutes each side. Halve the extra lemons and
griddle until lightly charred. Rest the steaks for 5 minutes while
you reheat the sauce. Serve the steaks with the puttanesca sauce,
some mashed potato and the griddled lemon halves.

Serves 4

grilled skirt steak with gorgonzola sauce

60ml olive oil
20ml Worcestershire sauce
2 garlic cloves, crushed
60ml dry red wine
1 heaped tbsp chopped thyme
1kg piece skirt steak
100ml single cream
250g Gorgonzola dolce*
1 tsp horseradish cream
1 heaped tbsp chopped
   flat-leaf parsley
roasted vegetables (such as
   potato and tomato) or rocket
   salad, to serve

Combine the oil, Worcestershire sauce, garlic, wine and thyme in a bowl. Season with salt and pepper. Add the beef and toss to coat. Set aside for 30 minutes to marinate.

Heat a griddle pan over a medium-high heat. When hot, cook the steak for 4–5 minutes each side for medium-rare (skirt steak can become tough if overcooked). Remove from the griddle and cover loosely with foil, then set aside for 5 minutes to rest.

Place the cream, cheese and horseradish cream in a pan over a very low heat, and stir until the cheese just melts. Stir in the parsley.

Slice the beef against the grain into 1cm-thick slices. Serve with the sauce, and roasted vegetables or salad.

* Available from good Italian delis.

Serves 6–8

beef fillet with quick **red-wine** sauce

40ml olive oil
4 x 180g beef fillet steaks, trimmed
2 onions, halved, sliced
2 garlic cloves, crushed
200g small button mushrooms, trimmed
2 tsp tomato paste
2 tsp plain flour
250ml dry red wine
375ml good-quality beef stock
mashed potato and watercress, to serve

Preheat the oven to 180°C/350°F/gas mark 4.

Heat 20ml oil in a frying pan over a medium-high heat. Season the steaks and cook for 2 minutes each side. Transfer to a tray and cook in the oven for 2–3 minutes for rare, 5 minutes for medium.

Heat the remaining oil in the same pan over a medium-low heat. Cook the onion for 5 minutes, or until softened. Add the garlic and mushrooms and stir for 1–2 minutes. Stir in the tomato paste and flour. Add the wine and stock, then bring to the boil. Reduce the heat to medium and simmer for 5–6 minutes, or until well reduced. Season. Remove the pan from heat and return the steaks to the pan just to warm through in the sauce. Serve the steaks and sauce with mash and watercress.

Serves 4

5 nights a week
lamb

lamb cutlets with lentil & fried-onion rice

2 heaped tbsp plain flour
1 tsp mild paprika
1 tsp ground cumin
1 tsp ground coriander
1 heaped tbsp mustard seeds
12 French-trimmed lamb cutlets*
40ml olive oil, plus extra to brush
2 onions, thinly sliced
200g cooked white rice
400g can lentils, rinsed, drained
1 heaped tbsp chopped flat-leaf
  parsley leaves
tomato chutney, to serve (optional)

Combine the flour with the spices and season with salt and pepper. Brush the cutlets with the extra oil, then coat each one in the flour mixture.

Heat 20ml of the oil in a large frying pan over a medium-high heat. Cook the lamb cutlets for 1–2 minutes on each side for medium, or until cooked to your liking (you will need to do this in batches). Transfer to a plate and cover loosely with foil to keep warm.

Heat the remaining oil in the same frying pan over a medium heat. Cook the onion for 3–4 minutes, until golden. Add the rice and lentils to the pan, stir to combine and heat through. Stir in the parsley.

Divide the rice and lamb cutlets among the plates. Serve with tomato chutney if desired.

* French-trimmed is when the meat has been cut away from the end of a bone to expose it.

Serves 4

greek lamb with crispy potatoes

3 garlic cloves, crushed
60ml olive oil
2 heaped tbsp chopped
   rosemary leaves
1 lemon, sliced
4 x 4-cutlet lamb racks
10 new potatoes
150g vine-ripened cherry tomatoes
160g pitted kalamata olives
good-quality mint sauce,
   to serve (optional)

Combine the garlic with 40ml of the oil, the rosemary and lemon in a bowl. Add the lamb, season with salt and pepper, and toss to coat. Set aside for 15 minutes to marinate.

Preheat the oven to 180°C/350°F/gas mark 4.

Meanwhile, part-cook the potatoes in a pan of boiling salted water for 5–6 minutes, then drain. Flatten each potato with a potato masher and place in an oiled roasting pan. Drizzle with the remaining olive oil and season well. Roast in the oven for 15 minutes, or until golden.

Meanwhile, heat a large frying pan over a medium-high heat. Sear the lamb on all sides. Place the lamb and any pan juices on top of the potatoes with the lemon slices and roast for 10 minutes for medium-rare, or until cooked to your liking. Remove the lamb, cover loosely with foil and leave to rest for 5 minutes. Add the tomatoes and olives to the potatoes, then return the pan to the oven for a further 5 minutes, until the tomatoes soften. Serve the lamb on the potato mixture, with mint sauce if desired.

Serves 4

herb-crumbed lamb cutlets

8 French-trimmed lamb cutlets*
80g (about 4 slices) white bread,
    crusts removed
2 garlic cloves
50g mint leaves, plus extra
    to serve
grated zest of 1 lemon,
    plus lemon wedges, to serve
85g feta, crumbled
60ml olive oil
12 vine-ripened cherry tomatoes

Preheat the oven to 200°C/400°F/gas mark 6.

Season the lamb cutlets with salt and pepper, then set aside.
Place the bread in a food processor and process to fine
crumbs. Add the garlic, mint and lemon zest, and process
until just combined. Add the feta and 40ml of the oil, then
pulse until the mixture just starts to come together.

Heat the remaining oil over a high heat in a large ovenproof
frying pan. Add the lamb cutlets and fry for 1 minute on each
side. Remove from the heat and place a small mound of the
crumb mixture on top of each. Place in the oven and cook for
5 minutes, then remove the pan from the oven and dot cherry
tomatoes around the pan. Season, then return to the oven for
a further 2 minutes, or until the tomatoes just start to split.
Serve with lemon wedges and garnish with the extra mint leaves.

* French-trimmed is when the meat has been cut away from the end of a bone
to expose it.

Serves 4

lamb **biryani**

20ml sunflower oil
6 (500g total) lamb fillets ,
    cut in 2cm cubes
2 onions, thickly sliced
20 fresh curry leaves*
4 tbsp korma paste
200g basmati rice
750ml vegetable stock
2 heaped tbsp currants
coriander leaves, mango chutney
    and poppadoms, to serve

Heat half the oil in a large heavy-based pan or casserole on a high heat. Cook the lamb for 3–4 minutes, until just cooked. Transfer to a bowl. Heat the remaining oil over a medium heat. Cook the onion and curry leaves, stirring, for 3–4 minutes, until the onion is softened. Add the korma paste and stir for 1 minute. Add the rice, stirring to coat it in the paste, then add the stock and currants. Bring to a boil, then simmer on a low heat for 12–15 minutes, stirring often, until the rice is tender. Stir in the lamb and heat for 2 minutes. Serve with coriander, chutney and poppadoms.

* Available from selected greengrocers.

Serves 4

lamb with **watermelon salad**

2 tsp cumin seeds
2 heaped tbsp fresh rosemary
1 tsp whole black peppercorns
½ tsp dried chilli flakes
grated zest of 1 lemon
grated zest of 1 orange
100ml extra virgin olive oil
4 x 200g lamb loins, trimmed
4 tbsp mint leaves, chopped
95g thick Greek yoghurt

watermelon salad
20ml olive oil
20ml lemon juice
300g watermelon flesh,
   roughly chopped
120g feta, crumbled
25g mint leaves, sliced if large
80g pitted kalamata olives, sliced

Pound the cumin, rosemary, peppercorns, chilli and 1 teaspoon salt in a mortar with a pestle, until coarsely ground. Add the lemon and orange zest, then stir in the oil. Place the lamb in a shallow dish, pour over the marinade, then turn to coat well. Cover and refrigerate for 2 hours.

Preheat the oven to 200°C/400°F/gas mark 6.

Heat a heavy-based frying pan over a medium-high heat. In two batches, sear the lamb on all sides, turning, for 2–3 minutes. Transfer the lamb to a baking tray, then roast in the oven for 7 minutes for medium-rare, or until cooked to your liking. Set aside for 5 minutes to rest.

Meanwhile, for the watermelon salad, whisk together the oil and lemon juice, then season and toss in a large bowl with the remaining ingredients. Stir the mint into the yoghurt and season well. Slice the lamb and serve with the watermelon salad and minted yoghurt on the side.

Serves 4

5 nights a week
pork

pinchitos with parsley & almond salad

pinch of saffron threads
2 tsp each coriander seeds,
   cumin seeds and fennel seeds
4 garlic cloves
2 tsp smoked paprika (pimentón)*
2 tsp dried oregano
1 bay leaf
40ml red wine vinegar
80ml olive oil
1kg pork fillets, cut into 1.5cm cubes

parsley & almond salad
500g broad beans*, podded
80ml olive oil
grated zest and juice of 1 lemon,
   plus wedges, to serve
1 bunch torn flat-leaf parsley
50g small mint leaves
6 spring onions, sliced
1 small green chilli, deseeded, chopped
2 heaped tbsp slivered almonds,
   toasted

Soak the saffron in 20ml boiling water for 10 minutes.

Meanwhile, warm the seeds in a dry frying pan over a medium heat, shaking, for 1 minute until fragrant. Place in a mortar, then pound with a pestle to a paste with the garlic and 1 teaspoon salt. Combine in a large bowl with the remaining ingredients, except the pork. Add the pork and toss to coat. Cover and marinate in the fridge for 2 hours.

Meanwhile, soak 24 x 12cm wooden skewers in cold water for 1 hour.

For the salad, cook the broad beans in boiling salted water for 3 minutes, then drain. Cool slightly, then remove the tough outer skins. In a bowl, combine the oil, zest and juice. Season, then add the beans and remaining ingredients. Toss to combine.

Thread about 4 pork cubes onto each skewer. Preheat a barbecue or griddle pan to a high heat, then cook the skewers, in batches if necessary, turning often, for 3–4 minutes. Serve with the salad and lemon wedges.

* Smoked paprika is available from gourmet food shops and delis. Use frozen podded broad beans if fresh are unavailable.

Serves 6

pork fillet with apple sauce

80ml white wine
80ml chicken stock
2 heaped tbsp Craisins*
20ml olive oil
350g pork fillet, cut into 1cm-thick slices
1 large Granny Smith apple, peeled,
   cored, thickly sliced
2 tsp finely shredded sage leaves
100g thin green beans, steamed,
   to serve

Place the wine, stock and Craisins in a small jug and set aside. Heat the oil in a large frying pan over a high heat, add the pork and cook for 1–2 minutes on one side only. Turn the meat, add the apple and cook for a further 1–2 minutes, until the apple begins to caramelise.

Pour in the wine mixture and bubble for 1–2 minutes, until slightly reduced. Add the sage and season with salt and pepper. Place the beans on plates, top with the pork and apple and drizzle with the sauce.

*Craisins (sweetened dried cranberries) are available from selected supermarkets.

Serves 2

quick **mu shu** pork

40ml peanut or canola oil
600g pork stir-fry strips
60ml reduced-salt soy sauce
40ml Chinese rice wine*
40ml oyster sauce
1 large carrot, cut into
    thin matchsticks
1 red pepper, thinly sliced
100g fresh shiitake
    mushrooms, sliced
6 spring onions, thinly sliced on the
    diagonal, plus extra to serve
¼ small Chinese cabbage (wombok),
    finely shredded (to give 200g)
2 tsp sesame oil

Traditionally this northern Chinese dish is served in Peking pancakes (available, frozen, from Asian food shops).

Heat 2 teaspoons of peanut oil in a wok over a high heat. Stir-fry half the pork for 1 minute, or until browned. Transfer to a bowl. Repeat with another 2 teaspoons of peanut oil and the remaining pork. Add the soy sauce, wine and oyster sauce to the pork in the bowl.

Heat the remaining peanut oil over a high heat. Stir-fry the carrot, red pepper and shiitakes for 1½ minutes. Add the spring onion, cabbage and pork mixture and stir-fry for 2 minutes, or until the liquid is almost evaporated and the cabbage has just wilted. Remove from the heat, stir in the sesame oil and serve topped with extra spring onion.

* Chinese rice wine (shaohsing) is available from Asian supermarkets. Substitute dry sherry.

Serves 4

pork cutlets with cranberry wine sauce

4 pork cutlets, trimmed of fat
20ml olive oil
2 garlic cloves, crushed
250ml dry white wine
250ml whole-berry cranberry sauce
1 heaped tbsp thinly sliced
   sage leaves
1 heaped tbsp chopped thyme
flat-leaf parsley leaves, to garnish
mashed potato, cooked rice or
   crusty bread, and a mixed green
   salad, to serve

Preheat the oven to 180°C/350°F/gas mark 4.

Season the pork cutlets with salt and pepper. Heat the olive oil in a frying pan over a medium-high heat and fry the cutlets for 2–3 minutes on each side, or until golden. Transfer the cutlets to a baking tray and cook in the oven for 5 minutes, or until cooked through.

Meanwhile, add the garlic to the frying pan and cook for a few seconds over a medium heat. Add the white wine and cranberry sauce and stir to melt the sauce. Allow to simmer for 2 minutes, then stir in the sage and thyme. Return the pork cutlets to the pan and coat in the cranberry-wine sauce. Serve scattered with parsley, accompanied by the mashed potato, rice or crusty bread, and a green salad.

Serves 4

pork **cutlet** with **orange** & **harissa**

3 oranges
500ml chicken or
  vegetable stock
2 heaped tbsp harissa paste*
2 garlic cloves, crushed
4 tbsp finely chopped flat-leaf
  parsley
4 small pork cutlets, trimmed
400g couscous
olive oil, to brush
50g pine nuts, toasted
wild rocket leaves, to serve

Preheat the oven to 180°C/350°F/gas mark 4.

Remove the zest from 2 oranges and place in a saucepan with the stock. Set aside to infuse while you prepare the pork.

Juice the 2 oranges and mix with the harissa, garlic and 2½ tablespoons of the parsley. Add the pork and toss to coat well. Set aside for 15 minutes.

Meanwhile, bring the stock to the boil over a high heat. Remove from the heat and stir in the couscous with a fork. Cover and set aside while you cook the pork.

Brush an ovenproof frying pan with a little oil and place over a high heat. Quarter the remaining orange, then cook the cut sides for 1 minute each. Transfer the quarters to a plate, brush the frying pan with a little more oil and reduce the heat to medium. Cook the pork for 1–2 minutes on each side, then return the orange quarters to the frying pan and place in the oven for a further 5 minutes, or until the pork is cooked through.

Stir the pine nuts and remaining parsley into the couscous, then divide among serving plates. Top with the pork, drizzle with the pan juices and serve with the orange wedges and rocket.

* Harissa (a Tunisian chilli paste) is available from selected supermarkets and Middle Eastern shops.

Serves 4

5 nights a week
midweek entertaining

fillet of beef with black-bean dressing

2 x 1.5kg fillets of beef eye
   fillets, trimmed
40ml olive oil
6 shallots, finely sliced on
   the diagonal
60g chopped coriander

black-bean dressing
15g canned black beans,
   rinsed, lightly crushed
2 long red chillies, seeds
   removed, finely sliced
2 tsp grated fresh ginger
1 tsp sesame oil
50ml soy sauce
30ml mirin*
30ml lime juice
120ml extra virgin olive oil

Preheat the oven to 220°C/425°F/gas mark 7 (or as high as your oven will go).

Tie the beef at intervals with kitchen string, tucking under the tapered ends to ensure even cooking, and season with salt and pepper. Heat the oil in a large frying pan over a high heat, add the beef and seal on all sides. Transfer to a baking tray and roast for 15–20 minutes (depending on how you like it cooked). Cover loosely with foil and allow to rest.

To make the dressing, place all the ingredients in a screw-top jar and shake well to combine.

Slice the beef and arrange on a serving platter, then pour over the dressing and sprinkle with the shallots and coriander leaves before serving.

*Available from selected supermarkets and Asian food shops.

Serves 20

warm duck salad with beetroot & pomegranate

8 baby beetroot
1 pomegranate*, halved
2½ tbsp redcurrant jelly,
   warmed gently
60ml extra virgin olive oil
20ml sherry vinegar
1 tsp Dijon mustard
4 duck breast fillets
100g thin green beans, blanched
60g baby salad leaves
   (or wild rocket)
150g marinated feta, drained
2 heaped tbsp chopped walnuts,
   toasted

Cook the beetroot in boiling water (or steam), for 20 minutes, until tender. Peel and quarter when cool enough to handle, then set aside.

Gently press each pomegranate half over a juicer to extract the juice and loosen the seeds. Place the juice in a bowl, then, using the sharp tip of a knife, remove the seeds and add to the bowl. Place the warmed jelly in a bowl and whisk in the oil, vinegar, mustard and 40ml of pomegranate juice. Season, then set aside.

Preheat the oven to 190°C/375°F/gas mark 5.

Heat an ovenproof non-stick frying pan on a medium-low heat. Season the duck and cook for 6–8 minutes, skin-side down, until most of the fat has rendered and the skin is crisp. Turn, cook for 30 seconds, then transfer the pan to the oven and cook for a further 5 minutes for medium-rare, or until cooked to your liking. Set aside to rest.

Place the beetroot, beans, salad leaves, feta and nuts in a bowl. Toss gently with 60ml dressing. Pile onto plates. Thinly slice the duck and add to the salad. Drizzle with the remaining dressing and sprinkle with pomegranate seeds to serve.

* Pomegranates are available in season from selected greengrocers.

Serves 4

spatchcocks with potato & bacon stuffing

20ml olive oil
5 rashers (250g) bacon,
    rind removed, roughly chopped
1 large onion, roughly chopped
2 celery sticks, roughly chopped
1 heaped tbsp chopped
    fresh sage
1 heaped tbsp chopped
    fresh lemon thyme
4 cold roast potatoes*,
    chopped if large
35g fresh white breadcrumbs
4 tbsp chopped fresh parsley
good squeeze of lemon juice
4 small spatchcocks*
50g unsalted butter, softened
cooked green vegetables
    or green salad, to serve

Preheat the oven to 200°C/400°F/gas mark 6.

Heat the oil in a frying pan, add the bacon and onion and cook over a medium heat for 5 minutes, until the bacon starts to crisp. Add the celery, sage and thyme, and cook for 1 minute, then add the potatoes, breadcrumbs and parsley. Season with salt and pepper and the lemon juice, then stir to combine. Spread on a tray to cool.

Stuff the spatchcocks with the mixture and tie the legs together with kitchen string. Rub the spatchcocks with butter, place on a baking tray and cook in the oven for 50 minutes, until golden.

Set aside to rest for 5–6 minutes before serving. Remove the string, pull out a little of the stuffing and place the spatchcock on top. Serve with the vegetables or a salad.

* Keep the cold roast potatoes from a Sunday lunch. Spatchcocks are available from supermarkets.

Serves 4

grilled squid with thai-style dressing

500g small squid, cleaned
20ml olive oil
1 small red onion, thinly sliced
200g baby salad leaves
   (or wild rocket)
1 long red chilli, deseeded,
   thinly sliced

thai-style dressing
110g grated palm sugar*
1 long red chilli, deseeded, chopped
1 garlic clove
5 tbsp coriander leaves
2cm piece ginger, chopped
1 tomato, peeled, deseeded,
   finely chopped
40ml fish sauce
20ml light soy sauce
80–100ml lime juice

For the dressing, simmer the sugar and 125ml water over a low heat for 2 minutes, stirring to dissolve. Leave to cool.

Pound the chilli, garlic, coriander and ginger to a paste using a mortar and pestle (or whiz in a food processor.) Stir into the syrup with the tomato, fish sauce, soy sauce, and lime, to taste.

Remove the tentacles from the squid, then cut the tubes open. Score a diamond pattern on the inside of the tubes, then cut into 5cm pieces. Toss all the squid in a bowl with the oil and 60ml of the dressing. Cook on an oiled griddle or barbecue over a high heat for 1 minute, until just cooked. Toss the squid with the onion, salad leaves, chilli and remaining dressing.

* Available from Asian food shops.

Serves 4

veal **saltimbocca**

4 x 130g veal escalopes
  (for schnitzel)
4 slices prosciutto,
  halved widthways
16 small sage leaves
40ml olive oil
40g unsalted butter
250ml white wine
buttered steamed baby
  green beans, to serve

Place each veal escalope between plastic wrap and pound with a meat tenderiser until about 5mm thick. Halve each flattened veal piece widthways, then season the meat.

Lay a piece of prosciutto on each veal piece and top with 2 sage leaves. Secure with a toothpick.

Heat the oil and half the butter in a large, shallow frying pan over a high heat. When very hot, cook the veal, prosciutto-side down, for 1 minute (you may have to do this in batches). Turn and continue cooking for a further 30 seconds, then transfer to a plate and keep warm. Pour the wine into the pan, bring to a boil and simmer over a medium heat for 3–4 minutes, until reduced, scraping up the bits on the bottom of the pan.

Add the remaining butter and stir to melt. Serve the veal with the sauce poured over, accompanied by the beans.

Serves 4

lamb with dukkah & spicy tunisian tomatoes

100g blanched almonds, toasted
60g sesame seeds, toasted
2 heaped tbsp cumin seeds, roasted
2 tsp za'atar* (optional)
20ml olive oil
2 lamb loins (about 300g each), trimmed

spicy tunisian tomatoes

9 vine-ripened tomatoes, quartered
2 long red chillies, halved lengthways, seeds removed, thinly sliced
12 spring onions, thinly sliced on the diagonal
1 heaped tbsp black mustard seeds
5 tbsp freshly grated ginger
8 garlic cloves, crushed
2 tsp each ground turmeric, ground cumin and sweet paprika
80ml olive oil
125ml balsamic vinegar
60ml red wine vinegar
75g firmly packed light brown sugar

To make the Tunisian tomatoes, place the tomatoes, chillies and spring onions in a serving bowl. In a separate bowl, combine the mustard seeds, ginger, garlic, spices and 1 heaped tablespoon freshly ground black pepper. Heat the oil in a large saucepan over a high heat until it's almost smoking and add the spice mixture. Stir vigorously for 2–3 minutes, then pour over the tomato mixture and stir. Heat the vinegars, sugar and 1½ teaspoons sea salt in a saucepan over a high heat until boiling, then immediately pour over the tomato mixture. Mix well and cool to room temperature.

To make the dukkah, crush the almonds, sesame seeds, cumin seeds, za'atar, 2 teaspoons salt and 1 teaspoon black pepper using a mortar and pestle until fine. (Alternatively, use a food processor, but do not over-process.) Spread the dukkah out on a sheet of baking paper.

Preheat the oven to 200°C/400°F/gas mark 6.

Heat the oil in a frying pan, season the lamb with salt and pepper and cook over a high heat until sealed on all sides. Remove and cool slightly. Roll the lamb in the dukkah, transfer to a baking tray and roast for 5 minutes, then set aside to rest for 5 minutes. To serve, slice the lamb and divide between plates and serve with the tomatoes.

* A spice blend available from Middle Eastern shops.

Serves 4

aubergine tagine

200g couscous
4 tbsp finely chopped mint
  leaves, plus extra to serve
40ml olive oil
1 tsp cardamom seeds
1 cinnamon stick
1 large onion, halved, thinly
  sliced
1 large aubergine, cut into
  1.5cm cubes
2 garlic cloves, crushed
2 heaped tbsp harissa*
400g can chopped tomatoes
125ml vegetable stock or water
40ml tbsp honey, plus extra to
  drizzle
4 hard-boiled eggs, halved
mixed salad seeds*, to sprinkle

Place the couscous in a heatproof bowl with 250ml boiling water. Cover and stand for 5 minutes. Fluff with a fork, then stir in the mint and season to taste.

Meanwhile, heat the olive oil in a large frying pan over a medium heat. Add the cardamom and cinnamon and cook, stirring, for 30 seconds, or until fragrant. Add the onion and aubergine and cook, stirring, for 3–4 minutes, or until the aubergine is golden. Add the garlic, harissa, tomato and stock and cook, stirring occasionally, for 8–10 minutes, until the aubergine is cooked through. Stir in the honey and season to taste with salt and freshly ground black pepper.

Spoon the couscous onto serving plates, then top each with some of the aubergine tagine and 2 egg halves. Sprinkle with salad seeds and extra mint, then serve drizzled with extra honey.

* Harissa (a Tunisian chilli paste) is available from selected supermarkets and Middle Eastern shops. Mixed salad seeds are available from greengrocers.

Serves 4

cinnamon chicken with bean salad

1 tsp ground cinnamon
2 heaped tbsp brown sugar
80ml dry sherry
80ml olive oil
4 chicken breast fillets
  (with skin and wing-bone
  attached, optional)
20ml balsamic vinegar
1 tsp Dijon mustard
200g thin green beans
2 x 420g cans three-bean mix,
  rinsed, drained
2 heaped tbsp chopped
  flat-leaf parsley
beetroot relish*, to serve

Preheat the oven to 180°C/350°F/gas mark 4.

Mix the cinnamon, sugar, sherry and half the oil. Season, toss with the chicken and marinate for 15 minutes.

Meanwhile, combine the balsamic vinegar, mustard and remaining oil in a large bowl, then season. Blanch the green beans in boiling water for 2 minutes, then drain and refresh in cold water. Toss with the dressing, parsley and canned beans.

Heat an ovenproof frying pan over a medium heat. Cook the chicken, skin-side down, for 2 minutes, or until golden. Turn and cook for 1 minute, then place in the oven for 12 minutes, or until cooked through. Serve the chicken on the salad, topped with beetroot relish.

* Beetroot relish is available from delis.

Serves 4

chermoula fish with pistachio couscous

4 x 180g thick white fish fillets,
    (such as John Dory or haddock)
200g couscous
250ml hot chicken or vegetable stock
2 heaped tbsp chopped flat-leaf parsley
2 heaped tbsp chopped coriander leaves
1 garlic clove, crushed
2 tbsp pistachios, chopped
400g can chickpeas, rinsed, drained
40ml lemon juice, plus wedges,
    to serve
harissa*, to serve

chermoula
3 garlic cloves
1 small red onion, roughly chopped
2 heaped tbsp chopped coriander leaves
25g flat-leaf parsley leaves
2 tsp ground cumin
½ tsp ground coriander
1 tsp sweet paprika
½ tsp dried chilli flakes
½ tsp ground turmeric
juice of 1 lemon
50ml olive oil

For the chermoula, process the garlic, onion, herbs, spices and lemon juice in a food processor, gradually adding enough of the oil to form a paste. Spread the paste over the fish, then cover and refrigerate while you make the couscous.

Place the couscous in a heatproof bowl and pour over the hot stock. Cover and stand for 5 minutes, then fluff the grains up with a fork. Stir in the herbs, garlic, nuts, chickpeas and lemon juice. Season to taste and set aside.

Preheat a barbecue or large frying pan to a medium-high heat. Cook the fish for 2–3 minutes each side, until just cooked.

Divide the couscous among serving plates, top with the fish and serve with harissa and lemon wedges.

* Harissa (a Tunisian chilli paste) is available from selected supermarkets and Middle Eastern shops.

Serves 4

moroccan pasties with roasted beets & carrots

80ml olive oil
1 onion, chopped
450g lamb mince
10 garlic cloves, unpeeled,
    plus 2 crushed garlic cloves
1 heaped tbsp ras el hanout*
2 tsp ground cumin
1 tsp ground cinnamon
1 heaped tbsp plain flour
375ml beef stock
120g frozen peas
2 heaped tbsp chopped
    coriander
1 bunch baby beetroot, halved
1 bunch baby carrots,
    peeled, trimmed
6 sheets ready-rolled puff pastry
1 egg, beaten
thick yoghurt and mint leaves,
    to serve

Heat half the oil in a large deep frying pan over a medium heat. Cook the onion for 2–3 minutes, until softened. Add the lamb and cook for 4–5 minutes, until browned. Add the crushed garlic and spices and cook, stirring, for 1 minute, until fragrant.

Add the flour and stir for 1 minute, then add the stock and season well with salt and pepper. Cover, reduce the heat to low and cook for 20 minutes, or until the mixture thickens. Add the peas and simmer, uncovered, for a further 5 minutes, or until the peas are tender. Stir in the coriander and allow to cool completely.

Meanwhile, preheat the oven to 200°C/400°F/gas mark 6.

Blanch the beetroot and carrots separately in boiling salted water, 5–10 minutes for the beetroot and 2–3 minutes for the carrots, until only just cooked, then drain. Place on a baking tray with the whole garlic cloves, drizzle with the remaining olive oil and set aside.

Cut six 15cm rounds from the pastry sheets. Use a rolling pin to flatten the rounds into oval shapes. Divide the lamb mixture among the pastries, brush the edges with egg and then press together to seal, forming a classic pasty shape. Place, sealed-edge facing up, on a greased baking tray and brush with beaten egg. Bake the pasties on the top shelf of the oven and the vegetables on the bottom shelf for 25 minutes, or until the pasties are golden and the vegetables are tender. Serve the pasties and vegetables with yoghurt, garnished with mint.

* A spice blend available from Middle Eastern food shops.

Makes 6

5 nights a week
indian

indian cauliflower & **chickpea curry**

2 tsp olive oil
1 onion, finely chopped
2 heaped tbsp medium-hot curry
    paste (such as rogan josh)
400g can chopped tomatoes
375ml salt-reduced vegetable stock
½ large cauliflower (about 500g),
    trimmed, cut into florets
400g can chickpeas, rinsed, drained
200g frozen peas
200g steamed basmati rice
1 heaped tbsp chopped coriander
    leaves
5 tbsp natural yoghurt

Heat the oil in a large saucepan over a medium heat. Add the onion and cook, stirring, for 5 minutes, or until soft. Add the curry paste and cook, stirring, for 1–2 minutes, until fragrant.

Stir in the tomatoes and stock, then bring to the boil. Reduce the heat to medium-low and simmer for 2 minutes. Add the cauliflower and chickpeas, simmer for 5 minutes. Add the peas and simmer for a further 3 minutes, or until all the vegetables are just tender. Season to taste with salt and freshly ground black pepper.

Stir the coriander into the yoghurt. Serve the curry on the rice, topped with a spoonful of the coriander yoghurt.

Serves 4

210 indian

tandoori salmon with cucumber & coconut sambal

250g thick Greek yoghurt
2 heaped tbsp tandoori paste
4 x 125g skinless salmon fillets
1 garlic clove, crushed
25g desiccated coconut
1 cucumber, peeled, finely chopped
40ml olive oil
ground sweet paprika, to sprinkle

saffron rice
300g basmati rice
½ tsp saffron threads
grated rind and juice of
   1 small lemon
2 heaped tbsp chopped coriander
   leaves

Mix half the yoghurt with the tandoori paste, coat the salmon and set aside.

To make the rice, place the rice and saffron in a saucepan of salted water. Bring to the boil and cook for 8 minutes. Drain and toss with the lemon rind, juice and coriander.

Mix the remaining yoghurt with the garlic, coconut and cucumber to make the sambal. Season to taste.

In a non-stick frying pan, heat the oil over a high heat and cook the salmon for 1–2 minutes on each side, until just cooked but still a little rare in the centre.

Place the rice in bowls, top with a piece of salmon and a dollop of coconut sambal sprinkled with paprika.

Serves 4

spiced indian lentils with raita

20ml olive oil
2 shallots, thinly sliced
2 tsp ground coriander
1 tsp ground cardamom
800g canned lentils,
    rinsed, drained
25g coriander leaves
2 tsp lemon juice, plus lemon
    wedges, to serve
steamed basmati rice and
    apricot or mango chutney,
    to serve

raita*
125g thick Greek yoghurt
½ cucumber, chopped
1 heaped tbsp chopped
    mint leaves
2 tsp lemon juice

Heat the olive oil in a saucepan over a low heat. Add the shallots and cook, stirring, for 1 minute, until soft. Add the ground coriander and cardamom, and cook, stirring, for 30 seconds, until fragrant. Add the lentils and 80ml water. Increase the heat to medium and cook for 2–3 minutes, until the liquid evaporates. Remove from the heat and stir through the coriander leaves and lemon juice.

To make the raita, place all the ingredients in a bowl and season with salt. Stir to combine.

Serve the lentils on the basmati rice with chutney, raita and lemon wedges.

* Substitute ready-made tzatziki.

Serves 4

pork tikka masala

20ml vegetable oil
1 tsp black mustard seeds
1 large onion, coarsely grated
5 tbsp tikka masala curry paste
600g lean pork strips
165ml can light coconut milk
250ml salt-reduced chicken stock
4 small courgettes, cut into batons
25g roughly chopped coriander leaves
steamed basmati rice, to serve

Heat the oil in a large, deep frying pan. Add the mustard seeds and cook over a medium heat for 30 seconds, or until they begin to pop. Add the onion and cook, stirring, for 3–4 minutes, until softened. Stir in the curry paste and cook for 1 minute, then add the pork and stir to coat in the paste mixture. Add the coconut milk and stock, then bring to a simmer and cook over a low heat for 5 minutes, then add the courgette and cook for a further 5 minutes, or until the courgette is tender and the pork is cooked through. Season to taste with sea salt and freshly ground black pepper.

Divide the curry among plates and scatter with coriander. Serve with basmati rice.

Serves 4

tuna pilau

20ml sunflower oil
1 onion, chopped
2 garlic cloves, crushed
1 heaped tbsp mild curry paste
  (such as korma)
1 tsp ground turmeric
1 red pepper, finely chopped
10–12 fresh curry leaves*
300g basmati rice
750ml vegetable stock
20ml lemon juice
425g can tuna in chilli oil, drained
60g mange-tout, thinly sliced
mango chutney and Indian pickle,
  to serve (optional)

Heat the oil in a large frying pan over a medium-low heat. Cook the onion and garlic for 2–3 minutes, until soft. Add the curry paste and turmeric, and cook for 1 minute, or until fragrant. Add the red pepper, curry leaves and basmati rice, and stir to combine. Add the stock and lemon juice, then bring to a simmer. Cover, reduce the heat to low and cook for 10 minutes, or until all the liquid is absorbed.

Add the tuna and mange-tout, and stir gently to combine. Serve the tuna pilau with chutney and pickles, if desired.

* Available from selected greengrocers.

Serves 4

5 nights a week
asian

teriyaki beef & beans

4 sirloin steaks (about 180g each)
400g thin green beans
1 large onion, sliced
40ml peanut oil
1 long red chilli, seeds removed,
   thinly sliced
coriander leaves, to garnish
steamed jasmine rice, to serve

marinade
125ml soy sauce
2 tsp caster sugar
80ml sake or dry sherry
2 garlic cloves
2 tsp grated ginger

Mix the marinade ingredients together in a dish, then add the steaks, turn to coat and set aside for 10 minutes. Blanch the beans in boiling salted water for 1–2 minutes. Rinse in cold water, then drain.

Toss the onion in half of the oil and season. Heat a griddle pan or barbecue to a medium heat. Cook the onion, turning, for 3–4 minutes, until charred and golden, then set aside. Shake the excess marinade from the steaks (reserving the marinade), then cook for 2 minutes each side, or until charred but medium-rare in the centre. Set aside to rest while you warm through the beans and onion on the grill. Bring the marinade to the boil in a small saucepan.

Cut the steak into thick slices. Arrange the beans and onion on plates and top with the sliced steak. Spoon over the marinade and garnish with the sliced chilli and coriander. Serve with steamed rice.

Serves 4

asian-style **duck** with **cucumber** & **radish** salad

1 heaped tbsp Szechuan pepper*
1 heaped tbsp garam masala
   spice blend
1 tsp ground ginger
1 tsp sesame oil
1 tsp wasabi paste*
grated zest and juice of 1 orange
40ml Chinese rice wine*
4 duck breasts (with skin)
30ml hoisin sauce
125ml chicken stock
steamed rice, to serve

cucumber & radish salad
1 heaped tbsp caster sugar
60ml lime juice
40ml fish sauce
1 cucumber, peeled,
   halved, sliced
1 small red chilli, seeds
   removed, thinly sliced
50g mange-tout sprouts
   or pea shoots

Mix the pepper, garam masala, ginger, sesame oil, wasabi, orange juice, zest and rice wine in a bowl. Using a sharp knife, score the duck skin in a cross-hatch pattern, then add to the bowl. Turn to coat in the mixture, then set aside to marinate while you prepare the salad.

Preheat the oven to 190°C/375°F/gas mark 5.

For the salad, mix the sugar, lime juice and fish sauce in a large bowl. Add the cucumber and chilli, then set aside.

Heat a large ovenproof frying pan over a medium-high heat. Remove the duck from the dish (reserving marinade). Cook the duck skin-side down for 2–3 minutes, then turn and cook for 2 minutes on the other side. Transfer to the oven and roast for 8 minutes for medium, or until cooked to your liking. Transfer the duck to a plate and set aside to rest. Drain the pan of excess fat, then add the reserved marinade, hoisin and stock. Allow to bubble over a medium heat for 2–3 minutes, until thickened.

Add the pea shoots or mange-tout sprouts and radish to the salad and toss. Slice the duck breasts thickly, place on plates and drizzle with the sauce. Serve with the salad and rice.

* Available from Asian food shops. Substitute dry sherry for Chinese rice wine.

Serves 4

stir-fried chicken with egg noodles

40ml oyster sauce
40ml soy sauce
40ml sweet chilli sauce
80ml stock
1 heaped tbsp cornflour,
  plus extra 1 teaspoon
400g thin egg noodles
½ tsp five-spice powder
300g skinless chicken breast fillets,
  cut into thin strips
40ml vegetable oil
1 each red and yellow pepper,
  seeds removed, thinly sliced
4 spring onions, cut into
  2cm lengths
2 garlic cloves, crushed
2.5cm piece ginger, grated
100g mange-tout
12 shiitake mushrooms
75g roasted cashew nuts

Place the oyster sauce, soy sauce and sweet chilli sauce in a bowl with the stock and extra teaspoon of cornflour. Stir to combine, then set aside.

Cook the noodles in boiling water for 10 minutes. Meanwhile, combine the five-spice powder and remaining cornflour, add the chicken and toss until well coated. Place half the oil in a wok over a high heat. Add the chicken and cook until golden, then drain on paper towels.

Add the remaining oil to the wok and stir-fry the peppers for 1–2 minutes. Add the spring onions, garlic, ginger, mange-tout and mushrooms and stir-fry for 1 minute. Return the chicken to the pan, add the sauce mixture and cook for 1 minute, until thickened. Toss in half the nuts. Drain the noodles and divide among bowls. Top with the stir-fry and the remaining nuts.

Serves 4

korean fish stir-fry

600g skinless white fish fillets
(such as John Dory or haddock),
cut into 3cm pieces
180g rice stick noodles
2 tsp sunflower or rice-bran oil*
4 spring onions, finely chopped
2 green peppers, thinly sliced
1 red pepper, thinly sliced
120g watercress sprigs

marinade
2 garlic cloves, crushed
1 tsp chilli powder
40ml soy sauce
20ml Chinese rice wine*
2 tsp sesame seeds, toasted
2 tsp sesame oil

Combine the marinade ingredients in a bowl, add the fish
and turn to coat. Stand for 10 minutes.

Cook the noodles according to the packet instructions. Drain.

Heat the oil in a wok over a high heat. Add the drained fish
(reserving the marinade) and stir-fry for 1 minute. Add the
onion and red and green peppers and stir-fry for 2 minutes.
Add the reserved marinade and simmer for 2–3 minutes,
until the fish is cooked and the sauce is slightly thickened.
Remove from the heat and fold in the watercress, then serve
the stir-fry on the noodles.

* Rice-bran oil is available from selected supermarkets. Chinese rice wine
(shaohsing) is available from Asian supermarkets. Substitute dry sherry.

Serves 4

char siu lamb with cucumber dressing

5 tbsp char siu sauce*
4 tbsp honey
60ml lime juice
6 x 3-cutlet French-trimmed lamb racks*
20ml peanut oil
fried or steamed rice, to serve

cucumber dressing
½ cucumber, seeds removed,
    very finely chopped
50g caster sugar
30ml white wine vinegar
20ml lime juice
1 long red chilli, deseeded, finely chopped
50g finely chopped peanuts

Mix the char siu sauce, honey and lime juice in a large dish. Add the lamb and coat well. Cover and marinate in the fridge for at least 6 hours, or overnight.

Preheat the oven to 200°C/400°F/gas mark 6.

For the dressing, put the cucumber in a sieve over a bowl, sprinkle with 1 tsp salt, then stand for 5 minutes. Rinse, then dry on paper towel. Place the sugar with 20ml of water in a small pan over a medium heat and stir to dissolve. Simmer for 2 minutes, then add the vinegar and lime. Set aside to cool. When ready to serve, stir in the remaining ingredients.

Heat the oil in a large non-stick pan over a medium-high heat. Add the lamb, fat-side down, and cook for 1–2 minutes each side to brown (they'll be quite dark). Place in a roasting pan, pour over the marinade and roast for 15 minutes for medium-rare, or until cooked to your liking. Rest for 5 minutes, then slice into cutlets and serve with rice, the pan juices and dressing.

* Char siu sauce is a Chinese barbecue sauce. It is available from Asian food shops and supermarkets. French-trimmed is when the meat has been cut away from the end of a bone to expose it.

Serves 6

5 nights a week
thai

coconut fish stew

20ml peanut oil
680ml coconut milk
250ml fish or chicken stock
60ml fish sauce
2 heaped tbsp brown sugar
600g white fish fillets (such as
    snapper or perch), cut into 3cm cubes
1 bunch choy sum, roughly chopped
juice of 1–2 lemons
coriander leaves, to garnish
rice vermicelli, prepared according
    to packet instructions, to serve

spice paste
1 lemon grass stem (pale part only),
    roughly chopped
4cm piece ginger, roughly chopped
2 garlic cloves, roughly chopped
1 long green chilli, roughly chopped
2 tsp chopped fresh coriander root
1 tsp ground cumin

To make the spice paste, place all the ingredients in a food processor and process until smooth.

Heat the peanut oil in a wok over medium heat. Add the spice paste and cook for about 2 minutes, until fragrant.

Add the coconut milk, chicken stock, fish sauce and sugar, then stir to combine. Cook for about 5 minutes, until the sugar is melted and the flavours are blended.

Add the fish and choy sum and cook until the fish is just cooked through and the choy sum is just tender (about 2–3 minutes). Add enough lemon juice to balance the sweet and salty flavours to taste. Serve over the rice vermicelli, and garnish with coriander leaves.

Serves 4

thai **pork** stir-fry

20ml peanut oil
1 red onion, sliced into thin wedges
1 heaped tbsp finely chopped
  lemon grass
1 long red chilli, finely chopped
1 heaped tbsp finely chopped ginger
2 garlic cloves, finely chopped
500g pork mince
2 heaped tbsp curry paste
100g green beans, cut into
  5cm lengths
30ml fish sauce
40ml lime juice
1 heaped tbsp brown sugar
60g Thai basil leaves*
cooked thin rice noodles, to serve

Heat the oil in a wok over a medium-high heat. Cook the onion, lemon grass, chilli, ginger and garlic for 1 minute, or until fragrant. Add the pork and cook for 4–5 minutes, until cooked through.

Add the curry paste and cook, stirring, for 1–2 minutes, until fragrant. Add the beans, fish sauce, lime juice and sugar and cook, stirring, for 1–2 minutes, or until the beans are just tender. Stir in half the basil. Serve on the rice noodles topped with the remaining basil.

* Thai basil is available from Asian food shops.

Serves 4

massaman duck curry

20ml sunflower oil
1 onion, thinly sliced
4 tbsp massaman curry paste
2 x 400ml cans coconut milk
3 kaffir lime leaves*
1 cinnamon stick
2 heaped tbsp brown sugar
1 Chinese barbecue
   duck*, portioned
4 potatoes, peeled,
   quartered, cooked
40ml fish sauce
60ml lime juice
2 heaped tbsp chopped
   coriander leaves
steamed jasmine rice, flatbread
   and sambal, to serve

Heat the oil in a wok over a medium-high heat. Add the sliced onion and stir-fry for 1–2 minutes, until the onion softens. Add the massaman curry paste and stir-fry for 30 seconds, or until fragrant.

Add the coconut milk, lime leaves, cinnamon stick and sugar, then bring to the boil. Reduce the heat to medium-low and simmer for 3 minutes. Add the duck pieces and the potato and simmer for 5 minutes to heat through. Stir in the fish sauce, lime juice and coriander. Serve with jasmine rice, bread and sambal.

* Kaffir lime leaves are available from selected greengrocers and Asian food shops. Chinese barbecue duck is available from Chinese barbecue shops (ask them to chop the duck for you).

Serves 4

red **prawn** curry

20ml peanut oil
3–4 tbsp Thai red curry paste
1 heaped tbsp grated
    fresh ginger
2 garlic cloves, crushed
1 large red chilli, deseeded,
    thinly sliced
1 small red onion, thinly sliced
1 lemon grass stem
    (white part only), bruised
2 kaffir lime leaves*
60g Thai basil leaves*
60g coriander leaves
60ml fish sauce
20ml sweet chilli sauce
300ml chicken stock
125ml coconut cream
500g prawns, peeled
    (tails intact), deveined
30ml lime juice
steamed rice, to serve

Heat the oil in a wok over a medium-high heat. Add the curry paste, ginger and garlic, and stir-fry for 1–2 minutes, until fragrant. Add the chilli, onion, lemon grass, lime leaves and half the basil and coriander and stir-fry for 1 minute. Add the fish sauce, sweet chilli sauce, stock and coconut cream, then bring to a simmer. Add the prawns and cook over a medium heat for 5 minutes. Remove from the heat. Add the lime juice and remaining basil and coriander. Serve with the rice.

* Kaffir lime leaves are available from selected greengrocers and Asian food shops.

Serves 4

chicken & mange-tout
with thai dressing

40ml lime juice

20ml fish sauce

1 heaped tbsp caster sugar

1 small red chilli, seeds
  removed, finely chopped

20ml vegetable oil

300g skinless chicken breast
  fillets, thinly sliced

150g mange-tout, ends trimmed

½ small red onion, finely sliced

25g coriander leaves

25g mint leaves

For the dressing, combine the lime juice, fish sauce, sugar
and chilli in a small bowl. Set aside.

Heat the oil in a wok over a high heat, add the chicken and
stir-fry for 1–2 minutes. Add the mange-tout and cook for
1–2 minutes. Place in a bowl, add the onion and herbs and toss
with the dressing.

Serves 2

5 nights a week
hot puds

sticky **date** puddings

175g dates, pitted, chopped
1 tsp bicarbonate of soda
75g unsalted butter, softened,
    plus extra to grease
150g light brown sugar
1 tsp vanilla extract
170g self-raising flour, sifted
2 eggs
double cream, to serve

sauce
200ml cream
85g brown sugar
60g unsalted butter
2 heaped tbsp chopped pecans

Preheat the oven to 180°C/350°F/gas mark 4.

Place the dates in a pan with 180ml water and bring to the boil. Add the bicarbonate of soda and set aside for 15 minutes (it will bubble fiercely, then settle down).

Cream together the butter and sugar until pale. Add the vanilla and 1 heaped tablespoon of flour and stir to combine. Add the eggs one at a time, beating until smooth. Use a metal spoon to gently fold in the remaining flour and stir in the date mixture (it may look a little curdled at this stage).

Grease six 250ml-capacity dariole moulds (or madeleine tins) with butter. Pour in the pudding mixture. Bake for 25 minutes, until cooked through. Set aside for 5 minutes before turning out.

To make the sauce, mix the ingredients in a pan over a low heat until the butter has melted. Cool slightly before pouring over the puddings. Serve with the cream.

Serves 6

apple, berry & port crumbles

50g unsalted butter
1kg Granny Smith apples, peeled,
   cored, cut into 1cm slices
500g frozen mixed berries
185g caster sugar
300ml port
½ tsp ground cinnamon
300g good-quality shortbread biscuits

Preheat the oven to 180°C/350°F/gas mark 4.

Melt 20g of the butter in a pan over a medium-low heat. Cook the apples, stirring, for 5–6 minutes, until soft. Add the berries, sugar, port and cinnamon. Cover and cook for 8 minutes, until the fruit gives off a lot of juice. Using a slotted spoon, transfer the fruit to a 2-litre pie dish or six 300ml ramekins. Reduce the juice in the pan over a medium-high heat for 3–4 minutes, until syrupy. Pour over the fruit.

Pulse the shortbread in a processor to form coarse crumbs. Add the remaining butter and process to combine. Top the fruit with the crumbs. Bake for 35 minutes, until golden.

Serves 6

lemon curd queen of puddings

60g unsalted butter,
   plus extra to grease
85g fresh white breadcrumbs
300ml milk
300ml single cream
zest of ½ lemon
3 eggs, separated
130g caster sugar
125g lemon curd

Grease six 200ml-capacity ovenproof dishes. Sprinkle the breadcrumbs into the dishes. Gently warm the milk, cream, zest and unsalted butter in a saucepan over a low heat. Beat the egg yolks with 60g of sugar until pale. Stir in the milk mixture, then pour over the breadcrumbs. Soak for 15 minutes.

Preheat the oven to 170°C/325°F/gas mark 3.

Place the dishes in a roasting pan and pour in enough hot water to come halfway up the sides of the dishes. Cover the pan with foil and bake for 20–25 minutes, or until just set. Remove the dishes from the pan and cool (this can be done up to 1 day in advance; keep refrigerated).

When ready to serve, whisk the egg whites until stiff peaks form; gradually beat in the remaining sugar until thick and glossy. Spread 1 heaped tablespoon of lemon curd on top of each custard, pile the egg whites on top, completely covering the base, and bake for 6–10 minutes, or until light golden.

Serves 6

quick pastry with berries & custard

2 (25cm x 25cm) puff pastry sheets
1 egg, beaten
110g caster sugar
300g fresh or frozen mixed berries
warm custard, to serve
icing sugar, to dust

Preheat the oven to 180°C/350°F/gas mark 4.

Cut each pastry sheet into four triangles, brush with egg and place on a greased baking tray. Bake for 15–20 minutes, until golden.

Meanwhile, place the sugar and 60ml water in a pan over a medium heat and stir to dissolve the sugar. Increase the heat to high and boil for 1–2 minutes. Add the berries and cook for a further 5 minutes. Allow to cool slightly.

To serve, place one pastry triangle on each plate, then top with some warm custard and a spoonful of berries. Finish with a second pastry triangle and a dusting of icing sugar.

Serves 4

warm **chocolate** cake

150g dark chocolate, broken into pieces
150g unsalted butter
100g caster sugar
5 eggs, separated
1 tsp vanilla extract
140g ground almonds
fresh raspberries, to serve

white chocolate sauce
85g white chocolate, finely chopped
125ml double cream
½ tsp vanilla extract

Preheat the oven to 200°C/400°F/gas mark 6, grease and line the base of a 22cm springform cake pan.

Melt the dark chocolate in a heatproof bowl over a pan of gently simmering water (don't let the bowl touch the water), then set aside to cool slightly.

Beat the butter and sugar until pale and light, add the egg yolks one at a time, beating well after each addition, then stir in the melted chocolate, vanilla and ground almonds. Whisk the egg whites until stiff peaks form, fold a little of the egg white into the cake mixture to lighten it, then carefully fold in the remaining egg white. Spoon into the greased cake pan and bake for 10 minutes. Reduce the oven temperature to 170°C/325°F/gas mark 3 and bake for 7–10 minutes; the centre of the cake will be quite molten. Cook for longer if preferred. Set aside to cool for 5 minutes before turning out.

Meanwhile, to make the sauce, place the white chocolate in a bowl. Heat the cream in a pan until just before it comes to the boil, pour over the chocolate and stir until smooth, then stir in the vanilla.

Cut the warm chocolate cake into wedges, pour over the chocolate sauce and garnish with raspberries.

Serves 6–8

5 nights a week
cold puds

oranges with **ginger cream**

6 oranges
375ml white wine
300g caster sugar
2 heaped tbsp finely
    sliced ginger
60ml Grand Marnier or curaçao

ginger cream
300ml double cream
2 heaped tbsp grated fresh
    ginger
3 tbsp icing sugar, sifted

Zest the oranges, reserving the zest, and use a small, sharp knife to remove the peel and pith, then halve each orange horizontally and place in a serving dish. Set aside.

Place the wine, caster sugar and 600ml water in a saucepan over a medium-high heat and bring to the boil, stirring to dissolve the sugar. Add the orange zest and ginger and continue to boil, stirring, for about 5–6 minutes, until the syrup has reduced by half. Remove from the heat and pour in the liqueur. Stir to combine. Pour the hot syrup over the oranges and refrigerate for at least 30 minutes to chill.

Meanwhile, to make the ginger cream, place the cream, ginger and icing sugar in a bowl and whip until soft peaks form. Refrigerate for 15 minutes to chill, then serve with the oranges and syrup.

Serves 6

little **fruit tarts** with **vanilla** cream

150g self-raising flour
2 heaped tbsp ground almonds
110g caster sugar,
   plus 2 heaped tbsp to sprinkle
80ml olive oil
125ml milk
125ml double cream
3 eggs
1 tsp vanilla extract
thin slices of tropical fruit (such as
   mango, papaya, kiwi fruit)
50g flaked almonds
30g unsalted butter, diced
icing sugar, to dust

vanilla cream
300ml double cream
35g icing sugar, sifted
½ vanilla bean, split, seeds scraped

Preheat the oven to 180°C/350°F/gas mark 4.

Grease six 10cm fluted tart pans. Combine the flour, ground almonds, caster sugar and a pinch of salt. Whisk together the oil, milk, cream, eggs and vanilla, then fold into the dry ingredients until well combined. Divide among the tart pans and place fruit slices into the batter. Sprinkle with the extra caster sugar and flaked almonds, dot with butter and bake for 20 minutes, or until golden.

To make the vanilla cream, place the cream, icing sugar and vanilla seeds in a bowl and beat until thick. Refrigerate until required. To serve, dust the tarts with icing sugar and serve with the vanilla cream.

Makes 6

'impossible' coconut pie

4 eggs
225g caster sugar
100g unsalted butter, softened
100g slivered almonds
100g desiccated coconut
2 heaped tbsp grated lemon rind
2 heaped tbsp grated
  orange rind
125ml lemon juice
125ml orange juice
250ml coconut milk
75g plain flour, sifted
lightly whipped cream and fresh
  passion fruit pulp, to serve

'Impossible' because it's just not possible to go wrong with this recipe. It's so easy.

Preheat the oven to 180°C/350°F/gas mark 4.

Place the eggs, sugar, butter, almonds, coconut, lemon and orange rind and juice, coconut milk and flour in a food processor and blend until well combined. Pour into a buttered 28cm pie plate. Bake for 1 hour, until lightly browned. Set aside to cool, then refrigerate for 1 hour to chill.

Slice and serve with a little whipped cream and passion fruit.

Serves 4–6

strawberry **soy panna cotta**

500ml strawberry-flavoured
  soy milk
1 tsp vanilla extract
50g white chocolate
3 (15g total weight)
  gelatine leaves*

compote
4 tbsp strawberry jam
200g small strawberries, hulled

Start this recipe a day ahead.

Place the soy milk, vanilla and chocolate in a pan over a low heat and heat until the chocolate melts.

Meanwhile, soak the gelatine in cold water until soft, squeeze out any excess water and place in a pan over a low heat, stirring until dissolved. Pour into six 150ml moulds or cups. Chill overnight.

For the compote, place the jam in a pan with 60ml cold water. Stir over a low heat until the jam melts. Add the berries and stir to coat in the jam. Cool to room temperature. Spoon the compote over the panna cotta and serve.

* Gelatine leaves are available from gourmet food shops. Always check the packet for setting instructions.

Makes 6

low-fat **berry tiramisù**

200g caster sugar
200g frozen mixed berries
250g low-fat ricotta
150g light cream cheese
1 tsp vanilla extract
375ml strong black coffee
60ml dry marsala
8 sponge finger biscuits (savoiardi),
  each broken into 3 pieces
1 heaped tbsp shaved dark chocolate

Place 130g of the sugar in a saucepan with 250ml water and stir over a low heat until the sugar dissolves. Increase the heat to medium and simmer for 5 minutes, then add the frozen berries and simmer for 2 minutes, stirring to coat the berries in the syrup. Remove from heat and cool completely (this part of the recipe can be made ahead of time).

Place the ricotta, cream cheese, vanilla extract and remaining sugar in a food processor and process until smooth. Place the coffee and marsala in a bowl and stir to combine. Dip half the sponge-finger pieces briefly in the coffee mixture, then divide among the bases of four glasses. Place 3–4 tablespoons of cheese mixture over the sponge fingers in each glass, then add some of the berries. Repeat with more dipped pieces of sponge finger, the cheese mixture and berries until all the ingredients have been used, finishing with a dollop of cheese mixture and a sprinkle of grated chocolate. Serve immediately.

Serves 4

index

picture credits

Soups pages 8-15
Macadamia Nut Soup Photography: Ian Wallace, Styling: Michelle Noerianto | Pistou Soup Photography: Ian Wallace, Styling: Julz Beresford | Spiced Carrot Soup with Coconut Cream Photography: Ian Wallace, Styling: Michelle Noerianto Minted Pea Soup with Smoked Salmon & Cream Cheese Toasts Photography: John Paul Urizar, Styling: David Morgan Bean & Tomato Soup Photography: Steve Brown, Styling: Julz Beresford

Salads pages 16-23
Lamb & Mint Salad with Potato Croûtons Photography: Mark Roper, Styling: Julz Beresford | Chicken & Wild Rice Salad Photography: Steve Brown, Styling: David Morgan | Taco Salad with Sour Cream Dressing Photography: Ben Dearnley, Styling: David Morgan | Prawn Caesar Salad Photography: Ian Wallace, Styling: Julz Beresford | Warm Squash & Goat's Cheese Salad Photography: Ben Dearnley, Styling: David Morgan

No-Cook pages 24-31
Lentil & Brown Rice Salad Photography: Ben Dearnley, Styling: Louise Pickford | Christmas Ploughman's Photography: Luke Burgess, Styling: David Morgan | Mediterranean Chicken & Couscous Salad Photography: Ben Dearnley, Styling: David Morgan | Deli Plate Photography: Mark Roper, Styling: Julz Beresford | Greek Antipasto Photography: Ben Dearnley, Styling: David Morgan

Something on Toast pages 32-39
Blue Cheese, Prosciutto & Rocket Bruschetta Photography: Ben Dearnley, Styling: Aimee Jones | Roast Tomatoes on Welsh Rarebit Photography: Ian Wallace, Styling: Louise Pickford Broad Bean Bruschetta Photography: Ian Wallace, Styling: Michelle Noerianto | Steak Sandwich Photography: Steve Brown, Styling: Julz Beresford | Crostini with Tuna, Lemon & Capers Photography: Ben Dearnley, Styling: Louise Pickford

Low-Fat pages 40-47
Poached Chicken with Pesto Photography: Steve Brown, Styling: David Morgan | Fish Baked in a Bag with Fennel, Tomato & Cannellini Beans Photography: Steve Brown, Styling: Jane Hann | Chicken Tenderloins with Baby Beetroot & Ricotta Salad Photography: Steve Brown, Styling: Jane Hann Salmon Spaghetti with Herbed Sour Cream Photography: Luke Burgess, Styling: David Morgan | Lemon & Oregano Lamb with Cucumber & Yoghurt Salad Photography: Ben Dearnley, Styling: Jane Hann

Kids' Favourites pages 48-55
Pizza Pie Photography: Ben Dearnley, Styling: Michelle Noerianto | Cheesy Tomato Risotto Photography: Mark Roper, Styling:David Morgan | Fish Pie Photography: Mark Roper, Styling: Valli Little | Cheesy Spaghetti with Bacon & Peas Photography: Ben Dearnley, Styling: Kristen Anderson | Chicken Dippers Photography: Ian Wallace, Styling: Louise Pickford

Eggs pages 56-63
Leek & Mushroom Frittata Photography: Ian Wallace, Styling: David Morgan | Soft Tacos Photography: Ian Wallace, Styling: Louise Pickford | Fragrant Egg Curry Photography: Ian Wallace, Styling: Michelle Noerianto | Coriander & Sweetcorn Omelette Rolls Photography: Ben Dearnley, Styling: Amber Keller | Moroccan Eggs Photography: Ben Dearnley, Styling: David Morgan

Peas & Beans pages 64-71
Spaghetti Bean Bolognese Photography: Ian Wallace, Styling: Michelle Noerianto | Pea Risotto with Prawns Photography: Ben Dearnley, Styling: David Morgan | Split Pea, Watercress & Goat's Curd Salad Photography: Steve Brown, Styling: Julz Beresford | Roast Chicken with Peas & Bacon Photography: Steve Brown, Styling: Julz Beresford | Four-Bean Soup with Barley Photography: Steve Brown, Styling: Kristen Anderson

Vegetarian pages 72-79
Spicy Bean & Chilli Fajitas Photography: Brett Stevens, Styling: David Morgan | Lentil & Vegetable Cottage Pie Photography: Ben Dearnley, Styling: Kristen Anderson Vegetable Tagine Photography: Catherine Sutherland, Styling: Valli Little | Cottage Cheese Pancakes with Roasted Pepper Salsa Photography: John Paul Urizar, Styling: David Morgan | Vegetable Samosa Pies Photography: Emma Reilly, Styling: Kristen Anderson

Stir-Fry pages 80-87
Beef Mince with French Beans Photography: Ian Wallace, Styling: Emma Garside | Pork Satay Noodles Photography: Steve Brown, Styling: Julz Beresford | Spicy Tofu Stir-Fry Photography: Steve Brown, Styling: Michelle Noerianto Chicken & Peanut Stir-Fry Photography: Georgie Cole, Styling: Michelle Noerianto | Five-Spice Vegetable Stir-Fry Photography: Steve Brown, Styling: Julz Beresford

Risotto pages 88-95
Avocado & Prawn Risotto Photography: William Meppem, Styling: David Morgan | Prawn & Lemon Risotto Photography: Ian Wallace, Styling: Louise Pickford | Prosciutto & Fontina Oven-Baked Risotto Photography: Ian Wallace, Styling: Julz Beresford | Duck & Shiitake Risotto Photography: Ben Dearnley, Styling: Kristen Anderson | BLT Risotto Photography: Brett Stevens, Styling: David Morgan

Pasta pages 96-103
Roasted Tomato & Chilli Pasta with Parsley Salad Photography: Steve Brown, Styling: David Morgan | Pumpkin, Sage & Ricotta Lasagne Photography: Brett Stevens, Styling: David Morgan | Simple all'Amatriciana Photography: Steve Brown, Styling: Kristen Anderson | Lemon & Basil Spaghetti Photography: John Paul Urizar, Styling: David Morgan Ravioli with Rocket & Balsamic Dressing Photography: Steve Brown, Styling: Julz Beresford

Pastry pages 104-111
Rustic Cheese, Egg & Bacon Pie Photography: Ben Dearnley, Styling: David Morgan | Sausage Pastry & Quick Chilli Sauce Photography: Ben Dearnley, Styling: Kristen Anderson Four-Cheese Galette Photography: Jason Capobianco, Styling: Michelle Noerianto | Salmon Wellington Photography: Steve Brown, Styling: Kristen Anderson | Fig & Three-Cheese Tart Photography: Steve Brown, Styling: David Morgan

Pizza pages 112-119
Prosciutto, Rocket & Tomato Pizza Photography: Mark Roper, Styling: David Morgan | Pizza with Melted Cheese & Lemon Salad Photography: Mark Roper, Styling: Julz Beresford | Spicy Pepperoni Pizza Photography: Emma Reilly, Styling: Kristen Anderson | Egg & Bacon Pizzas Photography: Catherine Sutherland, Styling: Valli Little | Maple-Glazed Squash & Blue Cheese Pizzas Photography: Ben Dearnley, Styling: David Morgan

Sausages pages 120-127
Maple Bangers & Mustard Mash Photography: Ben Dearnley, Styling: David Morgan | Sausage, Pea & Feta Salad Photography: Brett Stevens, Styling: David Morgan Spicy Stuffed Sausage & Cheese Croissants Photography: Ian Wallace, Styling: Louise Pickford | Rigatoni Milano Photography: Brett Stevens, Styling: David Morgan Barbecued Frankfurters with Coleslaw Photography: John Paul Urizar, Styling: David Morgan

Mince pages 128-135
Rice Noodles with Sweet-Chilli Meatballs Photography: Ben Dearnley, Styling: David Morgan | Chilli Beef On Avocado Photography: Ben Dearnley, Styling: David Morgan | Satay Beef Lettuce Parcels Photography: Steve Brown, Styling: Jane Hann | Home-Style Doner Kebab Photography: Ben Dearnley, Styling: David Morgan | Quick Pasta & Meatballs Photography: Catherine Sutherland, Styling: Valli Little

Burgers pages 136-143
Tuscan Burgers Photography: Ben Dearnley, Styling: Julz Beresford | Mushroom & Goat's Cheese Panini Photography: Ian Wallace, Styling: Michelle Noerianto | Lamb Burgers with Beetroot Salsa Photography: Luke Burgess, Styling: Julz Beresford | Curried Vegetable Burgers Photography: John Paul Urizar, Styling: David Morgan | Lamb Burgers with Feta & Tomato Photography: Ian Wallace, Styling: Louise Pickford

Fish pages 144-151
Swordfish with Italian Parsley Salad & Garlic Mash Photography: Brett Stevens, Styling: David Morgan | Sweet-&-Sour Fish with Pineapple Rice Photography: Ben Dearnley, Styling: David Morgan | Steamed Fish with Black-Bean Sauce Photography: Ben Dearnley, Styling: Michelle Noerianto Harissa Fish with Fattoush Photography: Ben Dearnley, Styling: David Morgan | Trout with Dill Potatoes & Beetroot Pesto Photography: Ben Dearnley, Styling: David Morgan

Seafood pages 152-159
Thai-Style Bouillabaisse Photography: Ben Dearnley, Styling: David Morgan | Seafood Stew with Rouille Photography: Ben Dearnley, Styling: Michelle Noerianto | Sushi Rice & Prawn Salad Photography: Steve Brown, Styling: Jane Hann | Easy Seafood Laksa Photography: Ian Wallace, Styling: Michelle Noerianto | Tikka Prawns with Yoghurt Pilaf Photography: Steve Brown, Styling: David Morgan

Chicken pages 160-167
Easy Chicken & Artichoke Rice Photography: John Paul Urizar, Styling: David Morgan | Chicken Tonnato Photography: Ian Wallace, Styling: Michelle Noerianto | Chicken & Pepper Tortillas Photography: Steve Brown, Styling: Michelle Noerianto | Chicken Pizzaiola Photography: Mark Roper, Styling: David Morgan | Chicken with Avocado & Pink Grapefruit Salad Photography: Brett Stevens, Styling: David Morgan

Beef pages 168-175
Quick Beef Stroganoff Photography: Steve Brown, Styling: Michelle Noerianto | Beef Braciole Photography: Ben Dearnley, Styling: David Morgan | Steak with Lemony Puttanesca Sauce Photography: Ben Dearnley, Styling: Michelle Noerianto | Grilled Skirt Steak with Gorgonzola Sauce Photography: Ben Dearnley, Styling: Julz Beresford Beef Fillet with Quick Red-Wine Sauce Photography: Ben Dearnley, Styling: Kristen Anderson

Lamb pages 176-183
Lamb Cutlets with Lentil & Fried-Onion Rice Photography: Emma Reilly, Styling: Kristen Anderson | Greek Lamb with Crispy Potatoes Photography: Steve Brown, Styling: David Morgan | Herb-Crumbed Lamb Cutlets Photography: John Paul Urizar, Styling: David Morgan | Lamb Biryani Photography: Catherine Sutherland, Styling: Valli Little Lamb with Watermelon Salad Photography: Mark Roper, Styling: David Morgan

Pork pages 184-191
Pinchitos with Parsley & Almond Salad Photography: Mark Roper, Styling: David Morgan | Pork Fillet with Apple Sauce Photography: Steve Brown, Styling: Julz Beresford | Quick Mu Shu Pork Photography: Steve Brown, Styling: Julz Beresford Pork Cutlets with Cranberry Wine Sauce Photography: Luke Burgess, Styling: David Morgan | Pork Cutlet with Orange & Harissa Photography: Steve Brown, Styling: David Morgan

Midweek Entertaining pages 192-199
Fillet of Beef with Black-Bean Dressing Photography: Ian Wallace, Styling: Michelle Noerianto | Warm Duck Salad with Beetroot & Pomegranate Photography: Ben Dearnley, Styling: Yael Grinham | Spatchcocks with Potato & Bacon Stuffing Photography: Ian Wallace, Styling: Michelle Noerianto Grilled Squid with Thai-Style Dressing Photography: Mark Roper, Styling: Julz Beresford | Veal Saltimbocca Photography: Ian Wallace, Styling: Julz Beresford

Moroccan pages 200-207
Lamb with Dukkah & Spicy Tunisian Tomatoes Photography: Ian Wallace, Styling: Michelle Noerianto | Aubergine Tagine Photography: Ben Dearnley, Styling: David Morgan Cinnamon Chicken with Bean Salad Photography: Steve

Brown, Styling: David Morgan | Chermoula Fish with Pistachio Couscous Photography: Emma Reilly, Styling: Kristen Anderson | Moroccan Pasties with Roasted Beets & Carrots Photography: Brett Stevens, Styling: David Morgan

Indian pages 208-215
Indian Cauliflower & Chickpea Curry Photography: Brett Stevens, Styling: David Morgan | Tandoori Salmon with Cucumber & Coconut Sambal Photography: Ian Wallace, Styling: Louise Pickford | Spiced Indian Lentils with Raita Photography: John Paul Urizar, Styling: David Morgan Pork Tikka Masala Photography: Amanda McLachlan, Styling: Kristen Anderson | Iuna Pilau Photography: Steve Brown, Styling: David Morgan

Asian pages 216-223
Teriyaki Beef & Beans Photography: Ben Dearnley, Styling: David Morgan | Asian-Style Duck with Cucumber & Radish Salad Photography: Brett Stevens, Styling: David Morgan Stir-Fried Chicken with Egg Noodles Photography: Ben Dearnley, Styling: Michelle Noerianto | Korean Fish Stir-Fry Photography: Ian Wallace, Styling: Louise Pickford | Char Siu Lamb with Cucumber Dressing Photography: Ben Dearnley, Styling: David Morgan

Thai pages 224-231
Coconut Fish Stew Photography: Ben Dearnley, Styling: Amber Keller | Thai Pork Stir-Fry Photography: Brett Stevens, Styling: David Morgan | Massaman Duck Curry Photography: Brett Stevens, Styling: Yael Grinham | Red Prawn Curry Photography: Steve Brown, Styling: David Morgan | Chicken & Mange-tout with Thai Dressing Photography: Ian Wallace, Styling: Lousie Pickford

Hot Puds pages 232-239
Sticky Date Puddings Photography: Jared Fowler | Apple, Berry & Port Crumbles Photography: Ben Dearnley, Styling: Jo Carmichael | Lemon Butter Queen of Puddings Photography: Ian Wallace, Styling: Michelle Noerianto Quick Pastry with Berries & Custard Photography: Ben Dearnley, Styling: Michelle Noerianto | Warm Chocolate Cake Photography: Ian Wallace, Styling: Michelle Noerianto

Cold Puds pages 240-247
Oranges with Ginger Cream Photography: Ben Dearnley, Styling: Michelle Noerianto | Little Fruit Tarts with Vanilla Cream Photography: Ian Wallace, Styling: Michelle Noerianto "Impossible" Coconut Pie Photography: Georgie Cole, Styling: Michelle Noerianto | Strawberry Soy Panna Cotta Photography: Ian Wallace, Styling: Louise Pickford | Low-Fat Berry Tiramisù Photography: Mark Roper, Styling: Julz Beresford

Recipe development
Nancy Duran: Minted Pea Soup with Smoked Salmon & Cream Cheese Toasts 12; Leek & Mushroom Frittata 57; Chicken & Peanut Stir-Fry 85; Prosciutto & Fontina Oven-Baked Risotto 92; Spiced Indian Lentils with Raita 212; Coconut Fish Stew 225
Kate Tait: Chicken Tenderloins with Baby Beetroot & Ricotta Salad 44; Lemon & Oregano Lamb with Cucumber & Yoghurt Salad 47; Soft Tacos 58; Split Pea, Watercress & Goat's Curd Salad 68; Four-Bean Soup with Barley 71; Sushi Rice & Prawn Salad 156; Beef Braciole 170; Quick Mu Shu Pork 188; Indian Cauliflower & Chickpea Curry 209; Pork Tikka Masala 213; Korean Fish Stir-Fry 221
Chrissy Freer: Steak Sandwich 37; Pork Fillet with Apple Sauce 186; Chicken & Mange-tout with Thai Dressing 231

When it comes to acknowledging people, it's difficult to know where to start, as there are always so many involved in the life of a new cookbook. Firstly, I'm very thankful to Tony Kendall and Sandra Hook at News Magazines for giving me the opportunity to produce another delicious. title in the '5' series. To Trudi Jenkins, editor-in-chief, we have both been with delicious. from the start and have enjoyed an amazing journey together. To the talented delicious. editorial team, you all play such a special part in pulling together the magazine each month – editor Sarah Nicholson, Danielle Oppermann, Amira Georgy, Sarah Macdonald, Alison Pickel, Simon Martin and our brilliant creative director Scott Cassidy. And a special thank you to Dan Peterson who, with Effie Nastoulis, had the huge job of collating all the shots and recipes once they had been selected. To the dedicated, hard-working food team, Kate Nichols and Olivia Andrews, it is my sincere pleasure to work with you. I also owe a world of gratitude to the photographers and stylists that I have the privilege to work with on a daily basis, your talent and vision is integral to the success of delicious. And thanks for the unwavering support of our friends at the ABC, particularly Stuart and Brigitta.

To the wonderful team at Quadrille, in particular Alison, Jane and Laura, who could see the potential of turning the beautiful pages of delicious. into an internationally successful cookbook, and who guided me through the process of putting it together (all the late night phone calls were worth it!).

Finally, I must thank my family: without your love and support, there would be no inspiration to cook.

First published in 2008 by
Quadrille Publishing Limited
Alhambra House
27-31 Charing Cross Road
London WC2H 0LS

Text © 2008 ABC/FPC
Photographs © 2008 The photographers
(For a full list of photographers see page 253)
Design and layout copyright © 2008 Quadrille
Publishing Ltd

Editorial director: Jane O'Shea
Creative director: Helen Lewis
Designer: Mary Staples
Project editor: Laura Herring
Production: Bridget Fish

Cataloguing in Publication Data: a catalogue record
for this book is available from the British Library.

ISBN 978 184400 589 5

10 9 8 7 6 5 4 3 2 1

Printed and bound in China